THE WORLD OF ROSES

THE WORLD OF
ROSES

By *BERTRAM PARK* O.B.E. V.M.H.

Chevalier du Mérite Agricole

E. P. DUTTON & COMPANY, INC., NEW YORK

First published in the U.S.A. 1962
by E. P. Dutton & Co., Inc.

© *Bertram Park* 1962

Composed in Baskerville type and printed by
Jarrold & Sons, Ltd, Norwich
Made & Printed in Great Britain

FOREWORD

Rosarians the world over look forward to a new book on roses much as fine chefs anticipate a new recipe. They may be familiar with all the basic ingredients, but they know that in assembling them in a fresh, new manner they may create a whole new taste sensation.

In Bertram Park's new book *The World of Roses* the reader will find that the ultimate in 'rose repast' has been attained. Mr Park, long regarded as one of the world's outstanding authorities on roses and their culture, has combined his equally famous talent with his camera in reproducing illustrations such as rosarians dream of on cold winter nights. The 128 full colour pages of illustrations from the standpoint of artistic talent alone warrant publication. However, each illustration is accompanied by vital information of great value to the rosarian. Such items as the American Rose Society and National Rose Society ratings, details of colour, habit, and disease resistance of each variety add a wealth of interest and value to this newest effort of Bertram Park.

Rose enthusiasts have come to expect great things from Mr Park. His two previous books on roses were widely acclaimed. His long service as editor of the National Rose Society's *Rose Annual* won him the admiration and esteem of rosarians throughout the world. In his newest venture Bertram Park has successfully attempted to include something for every one in roses. The reader is invited to view roses from the original species through the age of hybridization and development to the present time. Some varieties included are so new as to have just reached the general public. World-famous rose gardens are also pictured and described.

From every standpoint, artistically, educationally, or simply for pure pleasure, here is a rose book which has been needed. It will surely become a standard work in the library of the true rosarian.

MRS NAT SCHOEN
Past President
American Rose Society

ACKNOWLEDGMENTS

MANY OF THE ROSES included in this book were photographed actually growing on the trees, of which I have about three thousand in my garden at Pinner, but where my collection was not complete I should like to acknowledge with grateful thanks the facilities extended to me to work in the gardens and nurseries of my many good friends:

M. Armand Auberson of the Parc de la Grange, Geneva; Dickson's of Hawlmark at Newtownards, Northern Ireland; Señor Ramon Ortiz Ferré of the Parque del Oeste, Madrid; M. Jean Gaujard in Feyzin, near Lyon; Mr S. M. Gault, Superintendent of the Queen Mary Rose Garden in Regent's Park, London; C. Gregory and Son, Ltd, at Chilwell, Nottingham; R. Harkness and Co., Ltd, at Hitchin; Wilhelm Kordes, of Wilhelm Kordes, Söhne, in Holstein; M. André Leroy of the Parc de Bagatelle, Paris; Signor Q. Mansuino of Poggio, San Remo; Samuel McGredy and Son, Ltd, at Portadown, Northern Ireland; A. F. Meilland, Universal Rose Selection at Antibes; the National Rose Society's Trial Ground at St Albans; H. Nonin et Fils at Chatillon, near Paris; M. Perroud of the Parc de la Tête d'Or, Lyon; Dr Elvio Ricci of the Roseto di Roma, Rome; John Sanday (Roses), Ltd, at Bristol; the Sunningdale Nurseries at Ascot; Wheatcroft Bros, Ltd, at Ruddington, Nottingham; and the Director of the Roseraie de l'Haÿ-les-Roses, near Paris.

I should like, too, to express my gratitude to Sir Winston Churchill for so kindly allowing me to photograph the Golden Walk at Chartwell.

All but fourteen of the photographs were taken by me; for these fourteen I warmly thank Mr E. S. Boerner of Jackson and Perkins, New York (Plates 96, 97, 240); Miss Julia Clements (Plate 242); C. Gregory and Son, Ltd, Chilwell, Nottingham (Plate 92); Signor Q. Mansuino of Poggio, San Remo (Plate 218); A. F. Meilland, Universal Rose Selection, Antibes (Plates 78, 79, 117, 211, 213, 220); Mr Sam McGredy (Plate 118). I should also like to thank the National Rose Society for permission to use nine photographs which I took for them (Plates 37, 38, 51, 54, 70, 80, 143, 151, 241).

Finally, I should like to thank Mr Leonard Hollis, Editor of *The Rose*, for his valuable assistance in checking facts and figures.

B. P.

ILLUSTRATIONS

Some Famous Rose Gardens

INTRODUCTION

Oh, no man knows
Through what wild centuries
Roves back the rose.

WALTER DE LA MARE

No flower has given birth to more legend than the rose. It has been said that Cybele created the rose when, angry with Venus, she took her revenge by bringing to life something more beautiful than the Goddess of Beauty herself. Or was the poet Anacreon justified in thinking that when the foam of the sea gave birth to Venus the earth gave birth to the rose?

In Turkey they say that the rose, like rice, was born from the sweat of the Prophet Mohammed. A Latin poet wrote that a loving smile gave birth to the rose. Or perhaps it was this way: pining for Flora, who loved only flowers, Zephyrus transformed himself into a flower of such exquisite beauty that Flora found it wholly irresistible. The West Wind had become the rose. Flora and Zephyrus were one. Another story tells that the blood of Christ, falling drop by drop upon the mossy soil at the foot of the cross, brought forth the loveliest rose of all, that which is known as the Moss Rose.

Legend follows legend. From the Creation to Christ to Mohammed, from the Middle Ages to modern times, the romance of the rose has been a living part of our poetic heritage.

The history of the rose is just as romantic as its legend; no other flower has such a remarkable written record, beginning several thousand years ago. Even more remarkable is that fossils of rose-leaves have been recovered from chalk strata of seventy million years past, during the Miocene Age. These fossils have been found near Bonn, in Germany, and in Croatia, and in Colorado too. None of this, however, was the real beginning, and it is now believed that the rose originated in Central Asia, from whence it spread eastward to North America, and westward to Asia Minor and Europe. No wild rose has ever been discovered in the Southern Hemisphere or south of the equator.

From Western China, South-west Asia, and North America have come many valuable species to decorate our modern gardens, but very few indeed have contributed to the make-up of our modern roses. Of these there are only four which have been used for breeding by the hand of man or the agency of insects to create all the beautiful, modern, many-coloured, dwarf rose-bushes which go by the general description of Hybrid Tea. Four others only have further assisted in producing most of the climbers and those roses now generally classed as Floribundas, and only a few more have gone into the make-up of the modern shrubs.

A number of roses grown hundreds of years ago are still found in gardens to-day, and it is fascinating to try to trace them back to ancient times.

It has been said by some that the Cabbage Rose (or *Rosa centifolia*, as it was called by the Romans) did not arrive until the seventeenth or eighteenth centuries, and that it was 'created,' or hybridized, by the expert Dutch horticulturists of that period from four species—*Rosa rubra*, *Rosa phoenicia*, *Rosa moschata*, and *Rosa canina*. But this theory ignores the fact that the Cabbage Rose was well established in Southern France at that time under its local name of 'Rose of Provence,' or the Latin name of *Rosa provincialis*.

It has also been said that *R. centifolia*, so well described by the ancient Roman writers, was really a Damask Rose. The Damask Rose was certainly brought to Europe by the Romans, but to my knowledge no variety of large size has ever been recorded —like *R. centifolia*, having a "hundred petals." The Damask Rose has characteristically small to medium, and thinly petalled, flowers on moderately vigorous plants.

To-day we know that sex in plants was only beginning to be recognized, explored, and understood in the late eighteenth century. Could the Dutch have had some fore-knowledge of artificial hybridization? It is possible, though very improbable (because the Cabbage Rose was practically sterile in its later development). That a large rose of from sixty to a hundred petals could have been created by natural crossings or bud-mutations in such a short space of time is difficult to imagine.

Of one thing there can be no doubt: *R. rubra*, *R. centifolia*, and *Rosa damascena* originated concurrently, and quite possibly from a common ancestor in South-eastern Asia, and it is equally certain that at various times the Centifolia travelled as far as North Africa, and from there to Spain, and from there to Southern France; and in Southern France it made its second home, became naturalized, and came to be known as 'Rose of Provence,' or by the Latin name of *R. provincialis*. At a much later date it was taken via the Bosporus and Constantinople through Austria, Germany, and at last to Holland, where, by intense cultivation and chance mutations, it was vastly improved, but by no means fundamentally altered. Perhaps it is because of the fine Cabbage Roses that we see in such profusion in Flemish paintings of the seventeenth century onward that the Dutch are given credit for its origin.

R. rubra arrived in Europe a little later than the Cabbage Rose, carried by the Phoenicians and Romans, travelling by the same route. Forms of it were grown in Abyssinia and Ancient Egypt. During the later dynasties it was commercially cultivated for a great flower-trade with Rome. It is amazing to think of how those millions of roses were transported from Egypt in galleys, arriving fresh in the Roman markets; unfortunately, there is no record of how this was accomplished, though of the same period we have detailed descriptions of Cleopatra's palace, the floors of which were said to be covered inches deep in scented rose-petals. We know, too, that rose-petal beds were made for her guests to recline on.

The Romans undoubtedly introduced *R. rubra* to Northern France, although the Crusaders may also have brought it back again later. By the Middle Ages it was in extensive cultivation, not so much for its beauty, but for medicinal purposes, and for cosmetics. In that period it became known as the 'French Rose,' or *Rosa gallica*, and by this name we still know it.

R. rubra, or *R. gallica*, also came to be known as 'Rose of Provins' (as distinct from *R. provincialis*, or 'Rose of Provence'), for it was in the environs of Provins, not far from

Paris, that it was principally cultivated. By the time of Napoleon nearly every other shop on the main street of Provins was the shop of an apothecary. In these shops the rose-petals were dried and prepared before being turned over to the physicians and surgeons of the Emperor's armies, who came to Provins especially to obtain supplies. But these rose products were also shipped out of Provins to apothecaries in other French towns and cities, because in those days the rose offered the principal ingredients in a large number of medicines for countless illnesses—including indigestion, debility, throat and skin infections, and eye-troubles.

In the thirteenth century *R. gallica* was brought to England by the Comte de Champagne, better known as Edmund, Earl of Lancaster, who had been sent to Provins in the year 1277 to quell a revolt against the King of France. The situation was grave. The Mayor of Provins had been assassinated. There was no government. It was necessary for Edmund to take up residence for some time in Provins, where he became enamoured of the local rose, and when he returned to England he brought with him the red 'Rose of Provins,' which became the inspiration for the official badge of the House of Lancaster. (These stories are related at length by the French historian, Opoix.) It is this rose which appears on the arms of the Lancastrians as does the 'White Rose' on the arms of the Yorkists—a lovely white rose inspired by the Alba rose, which —John Gerard, the herbalist and superintendent of Burghley's gardens, relates—grew freely on the roadside hedges of Lancashire, and elsewhere in the North of England. Later the White Rose of York and the Red Rose of Lancaster were combined to form the Tudor Rose—the badge of the Royal House of England: a union which took place after the Wars of the Roses, when Henry Tudor (Henry VII) married Elizabeth of York. And so *R. gallica*, which had been brought to the North of Europe by the Romans, became a part of British history.

Another rose introduced by the Romans was the Damask Rose. It was cultivated in enormous quantities for the Roman markets. For one feast alone the Emperor Nero spent the modern equivalent of more than £35,000 (approximately 100,000 dollars) on roses. At Paestum, in Southern Italy, great nurseries were established for the cut-flower trade with Rome, and it was here that there was recorded for the first time an autumn-flowering Damask called *Rosa bifera*. Later it was called 'La Rose à Quatres Saisons' by the French. It is possible that this rose is the result of a bud-mutation caused by intense cultivation, and was found among the plants of the original species, but it is more likely that it was a hybrid brought from Asia Minor which had been crossed with a perpetual-flowering rose from China. There was a great caravan-trade between China, Asia Minor, and Persia in the later pre-Christian centuries.

By Christian times the rose had come to be severely frowned upon as a relic of Roman paganism. Gradually, however, it was not only accepted, but used in religious ceremonial, as it had been before in the service of the gods of Rome; and the rosary, the beads of which were originally made from rose-hips, reminds us of its far-reaching significance to Catholics. During the Dark Ages the cultivation of the rose, along with so many other aspects of civilization, declined, but the rose in all its forms survived— particularly in the gardens of the monasteries, where it was mainly cultivated for its medicinal properties.

In the early eighteenth century the merchants of the East India Company discovered a China Rose, *Rosa chinensis*, at Canton. They brought it back with them to Calcutta, where it was cultivated in the Botanical Gardens. Although it is said to have first arrived in England about the middle of the century, it appears to have been lost. It is recorded later at the Botanical Gardens at Haarlem, Holland, from where it was once more brought back to England by Sir Joseph Banks, about 1790.

The Damask 'Rose à Quatre Saisons' was crossed with Gallicas and other roses of the period, and these became quite a large class known as Portland Roses, named after the then Duchess of Portland. They were popular garden subjects up to the mid-nineteenth century, but, as far as I know, are extinct at the present time.

The Bourbon Rose, some varieties of which are still deservedly popular in modern gardens, is a cross between 'Rose à Quatre Saisons' and a China Rose. It is said to have originated in the Ile de la Réunion—or Ile Bourbon, as it was then known—in the Indian Ocean, as a natural cross between the Autumn Damask Roses, used for hedging purposes in the island, and a China Rose. It was discovered there by a French botanist, the curator of the Botanical Gardens, and sent to France. Since a similar hybrid is also recorded as having been known previously in the Botanical Gardens at Calcutta, its actual place of origin is uncertain.

This China Rose is of great interest as it was the first really perpetual-flowering rose to be introduced into Europe. The Damask 'Rose à Quatre Saisons' was, it is true, repeat-flowering—but only under favourable conditions, and by no means freely.

R. chinensis was never used for hybridizing to any great extent. Its progeny never became very important, and the original apparently became lost, and disappeared from cultivation in Europe. Quite recently it has been re-discovered in the island of Bermuda, and brought back to England.

Another Chinese rose, *Rosa odorata*, was brought to England about 1810. It has proved to be much more important as an ancestor. Similar in many ways to the earlier *R. chinensis*, it possessed the same essential characteristic that has given to all modern roses their quality of perpetual-flowering. This rose—a pale pink in colour—and a number of other varieties, arrived in Europe from Canton. Then, about 1820, there came a richly coloured buff-sulphur variety. The common name for all these *R. odorata* varieties was Tea Roses. This was because their fragrance was not unlike that which emanated from the tea-chests in the ships of the East India Company. All of these Tea Roses were far removed from their original species. They were semi-double to full-petalled, moderately large, and well-formed. They had probably been cultivated in Chinese gardens for hundreds, if not thousands, of years. No one knows. But they had been bred naturally, and by mutations from *R. chinensis* and other species. Paintings of them appear on many porcelains of the later dynasties.

The Tea Roses developed rapidly, and became very popular. In the nineteenth century a great many varieties, including climbing forms, were introduced. The principal characteristics of these roses are a beautiful form and pleasant fragrance. Very free and perpetual-flowering, they have a vigorous growth in a warm climate, and so are not seen at their best in Northern Europe. Most of them were bred in France, and have French names, and for a time they were great favourites in spite of their delicate constitution. Their foliage is almost immune to common rose diseases such as Mildew and Black Spot. They have ovate deep-green shiny leaflets which cling to the plant longer than do most, and their colours range from deep pink to soft buff-yellows. Reds and pure yellows were yet to come.

From 1840 to 1880 there gradually appeared many hybrids from all of the previous classes—the Gallicas, Damasks, Centifolias, Chinas, Portlands, and Bourbons. *Rosa alba*, a Northern European species, also came into the line, and brought some pure whites. In England this mixed and heterogeneous race became known as the Hybrid Perpetuals. But this is a misnomer. Though most of them did have some repeat-flowering, very few of them were actually 'perpetual.' Their colours had become rich and deep in reds and purples with many pinks; they had a vigorous and healthy constitution, but very few have survived to the present day. 'Frau Karl Druschki' is still very popular, but is only nominally a Hybrid Perpetual.

The next, and obvious, development came with the crossing of the Hybrid Perpetuals and the Tea Roses. Immediately the influence of the China Roses caused an increase of free-flowering qualities. Although the new hybrids lost some of the vigour of their parents and the flowers were often much smaller, they were more delicate in their beauty and the plants more decorative. In a few years they became predominant, and quite superseded their parents in public affection. They were known as Hybrid Teas.

Then, at the turn of the century, came the great revolution in the World of Roses. In the month of May, in 1885, M. Pernet-Ducher, a nurseryman of Vernissieux, near Lyon, was walking in the gardens of the Parc de la Tête d'Or in Lyon, when he saw a large bush of 'Persian Yellow,' and near by was the original species, *Rosa foetida*; and growing half-way up the main stem of this was a branch about five feet long, which was the copper-red-and-yellow 'sport,' named *Rosa foetida bicolor*, the species which became known in France as 'Capucine Bicolore,' and sometimes known in England by the false names of Austrian Briar and Austrian Copper. Seeing such magnificent specimens of these species for the first time, we can imagine his amazement. I, myself, was amazed a few years ago when, on the same spot, I rounded a corner of the garden to see the ten-foot-tall spreading bush shimmering from top to base in the sunlight.

R. foetida is one of the oldest roses known to be cultivated by man. In the ruins of the Palace of Knossos, Crete, over four thousand years ago, were found well-preserved wall-paintings with decorations obviously inspired by the 'Persian Yellow' rose, *R. foetida persiana*. True, the rose is shown with six petals; but this was artistic licence in a purely decorative design. It was introduced to Spain prior to the thirteenth century, during the Moorish occupation, and is reported in Holland in the sixteenth century, having been brought from Austria (hence its false name). Gerard describes it in his *Herball, or generall Historie of Plantes* (1597) as growing in his garden.

Now, when Pernet-Ducher saw this flaming bush there was no true yellow garden rose, nor orange-flame-coloured roses, nor bicolours. So he immediately decided to hybridize his roses with the pollen of these species. It was many years before anything at all promising was obtained. The crossings were not compatible. But he did manage to obtain a number of seedlings with the 'Persian Yellow' and crossed these again on to the same and other seedlings, in particular on to the 'Antoine Ducher' rose, a Hybrid Perpetual of violet-red colour. At last, thirteen years later, in 1898, there flowered for the first time a variety that approached his goal. He named it 'Soleil d'Or.' It was shown to a special Commission in 1899, and exhibited for the first time at the French National Exposition of Horticulture in 1900. Although not a pure yellow, it was of a shade hitherto unknown in roses; the outside of the petals was light yellow, the inside orange-red or pink.

Pernet-Ducher, naturally enough, was not satisfied, for he wanted to obtain the pure yellow of his pollen parent. Continuing work, he finally was able to send out, in 1905, the 'Mme Melanie Soupert' rose, a salmon-yellow similar to 'Soleil d'Or,' but much more yellow. Crossing this again with 'Soleil d'Or,' he finally produced and distributed the first pure yellow garden rose known to the world: 'Rayon d'Or.' That was in 1910.

Other hybridists were, of course, not slow to begin using 'Soleil d'Or,' and it was in the same year that William Paul developed 'Juliet,' a bicolour, the first rose showing true pure yellow to be sent out by an Englishman. In 1913 came the famous 'Madame Edouard Herriot' rose, which was the final result of one of Pernet-Ducher's crossings with the Foetida sport, 'Capucine Bicolore.' He exhibited this rose at the Summer Show of the National Rose Society of Great Britain, where, in a competition organized by the London *Daily Mail*, it won the first prize of £1000 and a Gold Medal. Later known as the 'Daily Mail' rose, it became one of the ancestors of all those brilliant orange-flame-coloured and bicolour varieties which are now so popular.

Raising more varieties with 'back-crossings,' but mainly working on his seedlings direct with 'Persian Yellow,' Pernet-Ducher came out with 'Sunburst' and 'Constance' roses, but it was not until 1920 that he created his masterpiece, 'Souvenir de Claudius Pernet,' named after one of his sons killed in the First World War. This was a full-petalled rich yellow, of perfect form, which has never been surpassed in a warm dry climate, but is not very hardy out of doors in Great Britain, and can be well grown only under glass. From these roses have come all the yellow, orange, and flame colours in all modern roses, and very few indeed of the roses in catalogues issued to-day cannot be traced to those roses of Pernet-Ducher in the first two decades of the century.

Climbing roses have also evolved gradually and been improved. Except for earlier hybrids apart from the species, they were all derived from *R. odorata*, *R. gigantea* (a climbing species native to Southern China and Burma), and *R. moschata*.

The last, commonly known as the Musk Rose, came originally from Northern India, and was known and widely distributed in Europe in the early nineteenth century, probably earlier; but the Musk Rose of Shakespeare was certainly not *R. moschata*, which was never naturalized in England. The "sweet musk-roses" which over-canopied Titania's bank in *A Midsummer Night's Dream* were almost certainly the common trailing or semi-climbing kind—the Field Rose, or *Rosa arvensis*, of the English country-side and open woodlands.

From *R. odorata* and *R. gigantea* came the early climbing Tea Roses and, combined with *R. moschata*, the Noisettes; but none of these hybrids is of great importance in modern gardens, except in semi-tropical countries where Tea Roses flourish. During the nineteenth century the Japanese roses, *Rosa multiflora* and *Rosa wichuraiana*, and their many hybrids and sports, were introduced into Europe, and have given us an important series of climbers or ramblers such as 'American Pillar' and 'Dorothy Perkins.' These, as well as all the widely grown climbing sports of the Hybrid Teas, need a great deal of the gardener's time and attention. Since the professional gardener is becoming scarce in private gardens, labour-saving varieties are becoming very much in demand. Great vigour of growth is no longer a prime consideration. Moreover, most of the vigorous climbers have only one crop of flowers. The modern demand is for moderately vigorous or pillar roses which will give a bushy well-branched plant up to ten feet or so, and will give perpetual- or recurrent-flowering all the summer.

A whole series of plants with these characteristics has been introduced in recent years. Such varieties as 'Dortmund,' 'Danse du Feu,' 'Aloha,' and 'Golden Showers' are the most suitable for the small garden. Where there is room for it, the perpetual-flowering 'Mermaid' rose cannot be surpassed as a climber, and the species *R. moschata* gives a wonderful shower of bloom, if only for a short season—rambling up and over trees, shrubs, and outbuildings. *R. multiflora* can be used, too, as an impenetrable hedge to contain wild stock. In America it is sometimes used as a crash-barrier at the sides, or along the centres, of the great trunk roads.

About 1920 an interesting series of shrub-roses was introduced by the Rev. J. H. Pemberton. These became known as Hybrid Musks, though they have little relation to the Musk Rose. This class was very little further developed until quite recent years, when Kordes, of Germany, introduced many varieties to fill the demand for large plantings of flowering shrubs in the many public gardens of that country. 'Heidelberg,' 'Bonn,' and also 'Nevada' (raised by Pedro Dot of Spain), are good examples of these varieties, and they are rapidly becoming popular everywhere.

R. multiflora also became the foundation of another very important class of roses. Crossed with Hybrid Teas and other sorts, it produced two distinct types, the once-flowering vigorous rambler and a dwarf perpetual-flowerer. (The former is the source of many of the ramblers at one time very popular.) To-day, however, they have been largely superseded by the more restrained growth and repeat-flowering qualities of the type similar to that created by Kordes.

The early dwarf varieties of Multiflora parentage, called Polyantha Pompons, were probably hybrids with *R. chinensis*, but other species and hybrids were used for crossing. This class consists of small flowers in clusters, and many of them open at the same time in recurrent-flowering. They are compact plants of about eighteen inches in height. Bushy, with small leaflets, they are almost without fragrance, but were nevertheless once very popular. They are now going out of production, and the modern Floribundas are taking their place. This evolution was begun by the hybridist Svend Poulsen, of Denmark, who, between 1912 and 1930, introduced a series of Polyantha roses crossed with Hybrid Teas which became known as Hybrid Polyanthas. This type was rapidly improved by the introduction of other hybrids and species; little of the original Polyantha remained. A new name, therefore, had to be found for this class, and the term Floribunda was first used for it in America.

These modern Floribundas are of moderate to vigorous growth. Those of moderate growth are best for bedding, and are in some parts rapidly ousting the Hybrid Teas in popularity, for they have still greater freedom of flowering, and have inherited from their ancestral species much greater hardiness and freedom from disease. They are becoming the choice of the businessman-gardener who must have the maximum of effect with the minimum of labour. Recently the form of the flower has greatly improved, and many, such as 'Papillon Rose' and 'Pink Parfait,' have clusters of perfect, small, Hybrid Tea type flowers. They are now called Floribunda Hybrid Tea type, and may be disbudded to one good flower on a stem, for cutting, or may be left to grow in full clusters, for better effect in the garden.

Shape of bloom is of even more importance with Hybrid Teas. The modern Hybrid Tea should be three to four inches across when half open. It should be of a regular shape. Each row of five petals should overlap, all the better if in a true spiral manner. It should also have a high centre. As the flower expands it should keep this good 'form' without blowing open into ragged confusion. To obtain this standard at least five or six rows of petals are necessary, and although a regularly patterned flat type or a completely confused form of flower may look well in a Floribunda, neither will do so in a Hybrid Tea.

The plants should be of moderate vigour so that they can, if desired, be pruned to be kept to a height of up to three feet; beyond this they would invade the shrub class, and be outclassed for freedom of flowering. A Hybrid Tea variety cannot normally have perfectly formed flowers of large size and have also the tall and vigorous growth and freedom of flowering of a shrub. ('Peace' may be an exception to this generality.) Important other qualities are a well-coloured and generous foliage, a strong resistance to the epidemic diseases of Mildew, Black Spot, and Rust, and sufficient hardiness to exist through a period of moderate frost without excessive protection.

Colour and fragrance are also very important, but are a matter of personal selection. All roses have some fragrance, varying greatly in intensity and kind, but one colour is missing from the rainbow of the World of Roses. This is pure delphinium-blue, which does not exist in the analysis of the existing rose pigments. By selective breeding, however, it may be brought in, for there are a number of mauve or lilac varieties. There is also always the possibility of a chance mutation producing the blue, just as a similar chance mutation produced the pure scarlet, and to-day the effect of X-rays or exposure to radio-activity could assist such a mutation.

In the past hybridists proceeded empirically in their experiments to produce seedlings which are an improvement on type. This still goes on to some degree, but in the future a scientific approach with basic research will be essential. To continually cross and re-cross our present hybrid varieties will not carry us much farther. New or little-used species must be brought into the breeding of new varieties. As happened in the early part of this century, a temporary decline in the quality of fragrance will be accepted in favour of greater resistance to disease which will follow the introduction of the blood of other wild species.

The life of any modern rose is short as a variety; there are comparatively few varieties in general cultivation more than thirty years old, and the life of the most modern rose of all, the yellow rose, to which we now return, seems shorter than any.

'Ville de Paris' and 'Julien Potin,' yellow roses of 1925 and 1927, have already been dropped from the National Rose Society's Select List. 'Phyllis Gold' (1934) is on the way out. 'Sir Henry Segrave' (as recent as 1932), a fine-weather rose, is very pale, and hardly worth growing in a normal season, but it did excellently during the wonderful summer of 1959. The most reliable of the older varieties is 'McGredy's Yellow,' as good as ever, although it was introduced twenty-seven years ago; in some districts, however, it is said to be declining slightly. 'Spek's Yellow,' of 1947, is the richest in colour of all the varieties, but the plants are 'leggy,' and, if pruned too hard to overcome this, do not last too long.

We think of so many recent yellow roses now—of 'Buccaneer,' 'Gertrude Gregory,' 'Belle Blonde,' 'Golden Masterpiece,' 'Gold Crown,' 'Golden Giant,' of the Floribundas 'Allgold,' 'Poly Prim,' 'Faust,' and 'Golden Fleece'—and of how much there is still to be done in the improvement of the yellow rose, in particular where resistance to disease is concerned, for yellow roses are very easily infected, owing to their tropical origin. *R. foetida* . . . what a difference it would have made to all our present-day roses had this been a hardier plant, like the only two other hardy species in the world having its pure yellow colour—*Rosa xanthina* and *Rosa hugonis*. *R. hugonis* is a large spreading bush, and comes from Central China, with its extremes of temperature, while *R. xanthina* is an erect, tall shrub from Northern China and Korea, where it is subject to even colder conditions. It would have made a great difference to our present World of Roses had these two fine plants been in the Parc de la Tête d'Or, in Lyon, when Pernet-Ducher walked there that day in May, in 1885.

The origin of the yellow rose is astonishing, and, for the reader who would like to think of it as a miracle, there is a charming tale related by Abel Belmont, in his *Dictionnaire de la Rose* (1896), that when the Prophet Mohammed waged war against the tribe of the Koreish, Mohammed's favourite wife, Ayesha, profiting from his absence, entered into an illicit relationship with a young Persian with whom she had fallen in love. Back in the town of Medina, the Prophet sent by God, suspecting unfaithfulness on the part of his beloved wife, consulted the Angel Gabriel, his usual counsellor. The Angel soon appeared in one of Mohammed's dreams, and said, "Ask Ayesha to drop an object into the pool in the centre of the seraglio. If she is innocent the object will remain unchanged. If she is guilty it will change its colour." The following day Mohammed asked Ayesha, who held a beautiful bunch of roses in her hand, to throw it into the pool. This she did, laughingly. Then, to the Prophet's chagrin and the amazement of all, the roses emerged from the water a beautiful saffron-yellow colour. When the episode came to light the pool became the object of great veneration on the part of the Moslems, and to this day it is the refuge of unhappy husbands.

The fact remains, however, that the development of the rose is the result of the patient work of hybridists all over the world. Every cross between two roses may produce many seedlings, and the same cross may be repeated thousands of times before the desired result is obtained. Signor Mansuino of San Remo, for instance, tells me that he made nearly fifty thousand crosses before introducing 'Purezza,' the white Hybrid Banksian climber. In Meilland's establishment at Antibes over forty-five thousand seedlings are raised every year. These are selected and re-selected over at least five or six years, until each year's crop of forty-five thousand is reduced to only three or four for a single year's distribution of new varieties. In California, U.S.A., at the Armstrong Nurseries, and at the establishment of Jackson and Perkins, there are acres of new varieties of roses under observation and trial every year, from which perhaps only *one* new rose may be selected for introduction to the outside world.

The rose, indeed, is an international flower, and in presenting this book I have envisaged readers in every part of the world where the rose is grown, from the Cap d'Antibes to the gardens of Lucknow, from California to Denmark. To these readers I offer what I like to think is a complete rose garden in colour. Most of my life has been devoted to the rose and to photography, and these photographs are, in a sense, the fruits of what has given me most pleasure for over thirty-five years.

I have tried to make my selection a representative one: the varieties shown are those which have received the highest international awards in their different classes. The photographs have been taken in many different countries—for which reason, incidentally, the expert may occasionally notice some of those slight colour variations which are dependent on soil, climate, and season.

To all those who love the rose I offer this book—hoping that it will give them pleasure in remembering past seasons, appreciating the present, and anticipating seasons to come.

1 FIRST LOVE

2 ETHEL SANDAY

3 LILAC TIME

4 JUNE PARK

5 WHITE SWAN

CHRYSLER IMPERIAL

7 THAÏS
(LADY ELGIN)

El Parque del Oeste, Madrid

8 SUPER STAR
(TROPICANA)

9 HELEN TRAUBEL

10 BRILLIANT
(DETROITER,
SCHLÖSSERS BRILLA

11 PICTURE

12 HECTOR DEANE

13 PINK PEACE

14 GORDON EDDIE

15 OPERA
(OPÉRA)

16 CONFIDENCE

17 RUBAIYAT

18 LAL

19 BACCARA

20 LADY ZIA

21 GARDEN PARTY

22 SUSPENSE

23 FRITZ
THIEDEMANN

24 DIAMOND JUBILEE

25 GAIL BORDEN

26   LA JOLLA

27   MRS SAM McGREDY

28 CHARLES GREGORY

29 MONIQUE

30 TALLYHO

31 SHOW GIRL

32 GOLDEN MELODY
(IRENE CHURRUCA)

33 MISS FRANCE

34 COPPÉLIA

35 CHRISTIAN DIOR

36 PIGALLE

37 CLEOPATRA
(KLEOPATRA)

38 SORAYA

39 MICHÈLE MEILLAND

40 JOLIE MADAME

41 BEAUTÉ

42 BAYADÈRE

43 MISS IRELAND

44 PICCADILLY

45 ROSE GAUJARD

46   MOJAVE

47   GERTRUDE GREGORY

48 ASTRÉE

49 GOLD CROWN
(GOLDKRONE)

50 MME KRILOFF

51 PRELUDE

52   DOROTHY ANDERSON

53   DR F. DEBAT
(DR DEBAT
LA ROSÉE)

SOUVENIR DE
JACQUES
VERSCHUREN

55 TZIGANE

56 MME LOUIS LAPERRIÈl

57 BETTINA

58 DUET

59 MISCHIEF

60 CHARLES MALLERIN

61 GOLDEN GIANT

62 GRAND GALA

63 McGREDY'S YELLOW

GRACE DE MONACO

65　FRED HOWARD

66 STELLA

67 SPEK'S YELLOW
(GOLDEN SCEPTER)

68 CHAMPS ÉLYSÉES

69 SYMPHONIE

70 MESSAGE
(WHITE KNIGHT)

71 SUTTER'S GOLD

72 MONTEZUMA

73 KONRAD ADENAUER

74 TIFFANY

75   PRESIDENT HERBERT HOOVER

76 PREMIER BAL

77 ANNE LETTS

PARIS-MATCH

79 SABRINA

81 SILVER LINING

82 GRAND'MÈRE JENNY

83 VIRGO
(VIRGO LIBERATIONEM)

84 EDEN ROSE

85 KARL HERBST

86 JOSEPHINE BRUC

87 PERFECTA
(KORDES PERFECTA)

88 MARGARET

CHARLOTTE ARMSTRONG

90   LADY SYLVIA

91   ENA HARKNESS

92   WENDY CUSSONS

93   LADY BELPER

94 CL. PEACE
El Parque del Oe.
M

95 PEACE
(GIOIA
GLORIA DEI
MME A. MEILLAND)

96 HAWAII

97 AMERICANA

98 INDEPENDENCE
(KORDES SONDERMELDUNG, REINA ELISENDA)

99   QUEEN ELIZABETH

100 MASQUERADE
(MASKERADE)

101 ROSEMARY ROSE

Regent's Park, London

102 GOLDEN FLEECE
(TOISON D'OR)
Le Parc de la Grange, Genève

103 ALAIN

104 PAPRIKA

105 CIRCUS

106 DEAREST

107 IVORY FASHION

108 SARABANDE

109 SWEET REPOSE
(THE OPTIMIST)
Regent's Park, London

110 GOLDILOCKS

111
RED FAVOURITE
(SCHWEIZER GRUSS, HOLLÄNDERIN)

112 VOGUE

113 AMA

114 FIRECRACKER

5 KORONA

116 MÄRCHENLAND

117 ZAMBRA

118 PADDY McGREDY

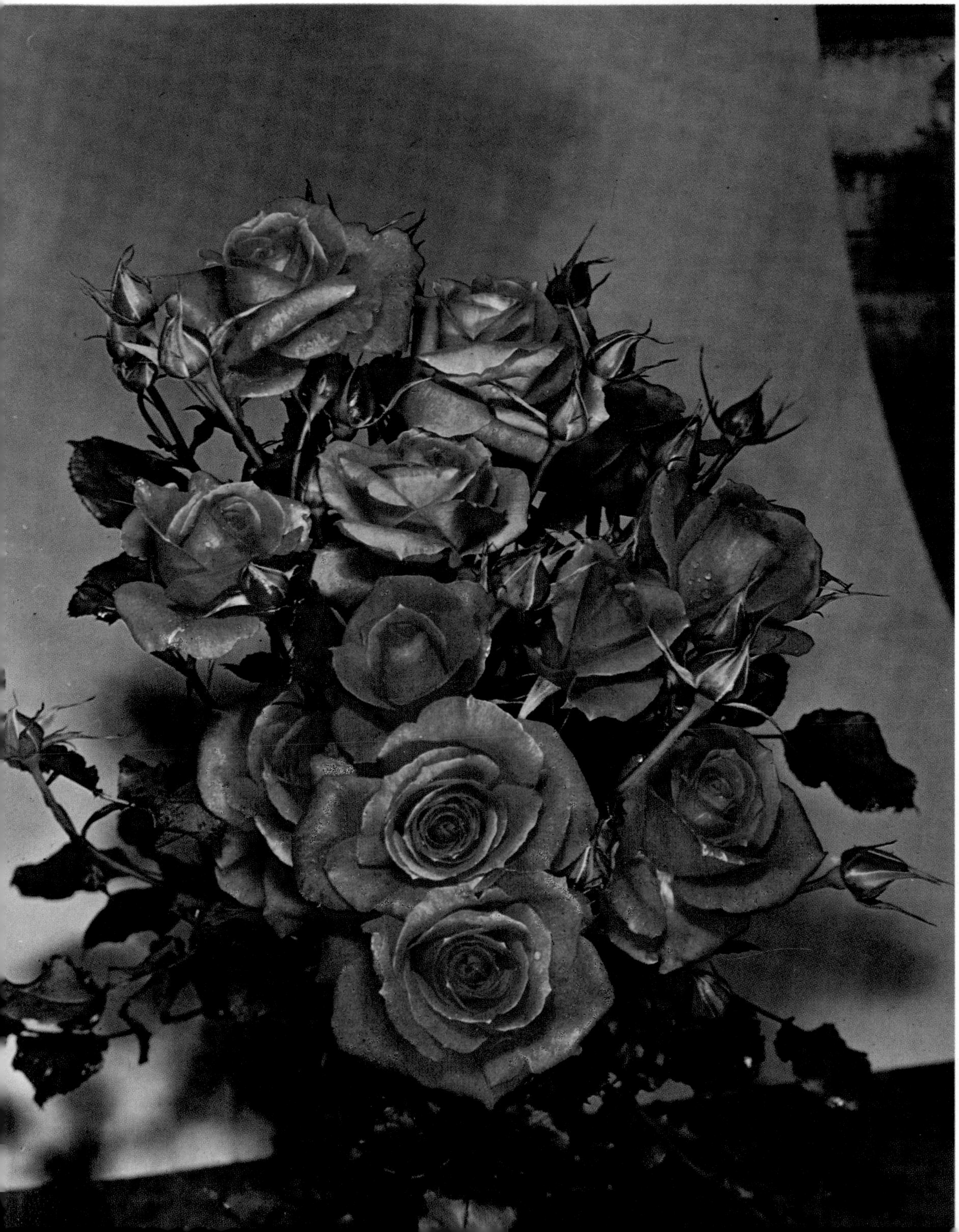

119 COCORICO

120 FAUST
(DR FAUST)

121 COLUMBINE

122 MA PERKINS

NE OF DENMARK

124 ANNA WHEATCROFT

125 POLY PRIM

126 LILLI MARLEN
(LILLI MARLEEN)

127 ELSE POULSEN

128 JIMINY CRICKET

129 GOLD MARIE
(GOLDMARIE)

130 MOULIN ROUGE

131 ORANGEADE

132 THE PEOPLE

133 DICKSON'S FLAME

134 MAGENTA
(KORDES MAGENTA)

135 ALLGOLD

136 FRENSHAM

137 BONNIE MAID

138 DAINTY MAID

139 ICEBERG
(SCHNEEWITTCHEN)
Regent's Park, London

140 RUMBA

141 AUGUST SEEBAUER

142 OHLALA
(OLALA)

143 YELLOWHAMMER

144
VAN NES
(PERMANENT WAVE
MEVROUW VAN STRAATEN VAN NES
DUCHESS OF WINDSOR
L'INDÉFRISABLE)

145 TIVOLI

146 PAPILLON ROSE

147 RED WONDER

148 PINOCCHIO
(ROSENMÄRCHEN)

149 FLAMENCO

150 GOLDEN JEWEL
(GOLDJUWEL)

151 BORDER CORAL

152 CHANELLE

153 ANGELA

154 SHEPHERD'S
        DELIGHT

155 KÄTHE DUVIGNEAU

156 FASHION

157 SPARTAN

BUCCANEER, OHLALA

159 COMMONWEALTH
(HERZBLUT)

160 PRESUMIDA
(LA PRESUMIDA, PETER PAN)

161 *ROSA ROULETTII*
(*R. CHINENSIS MINIMA*, POMPON DE PA

162
BABY GOLD STAR (ESTRELLITA DE ORO)
CINDERELLA

163 PERLE D'ALCANADA
(BABY CRIMSON, TITANIA
WHEATCROFT'S BABY CRIMSON
PERLA DE ALCANADA)

164 ROSINA
(JOSEPHINE WHEATCROFT)

165 MIDGET

166 TINKER BELL

167 LITTLE BUCKAROO

168 HUMPTY-DUMPTY

169 POUR TOI
(PARA TI, FOR YOU, WENDY)

170 BABY MASQUERADE
(BABY MASKERADE)

171 CORALIN

172 PETITE DE HOLLANDE
(PETITE JUNON DE HOLLANDE)

173 CARDINAL DE RICHELIEU
(ROSE VAN SIAN)

174 DUCHESSE DE MONTEBELLO

175 CELSIANA

176 CHARLES DE MILLS

177
ZIGEUNER KNABE
(GIPSY BOY)

178 *ROSA MUNDI*
   (R. GALLICA VERSICOLOR)

179 MME HARDY

180
CHAPEAU DE NAPOLÉON
(*R. CENTIFOLIA CRISTATA*, CRESTED MOSS)

181 MME PLANTIER

ROSA OMEIENSIS PTERACANTHA
(R. SERICEA PTERACANTHA)

184 *ROSA PRIMULA*

183 *ROSA WILLMOTTIAE*

185 *ROSA MOYESII*

186 *ROSA SPINOSISSIMA ALTAICA*

187 SARAH VAN FLEET

188 SCHNEEZWERG
(SNOW DWARF)

189 BELLE POITEVINE

190 *ROSA RUGOSA SCABROSA*

191 ROSERAIE DE L'HAŸ

192 HEIDELBERG

193 *ROSA ODORATA MAJOR*

194 FRÜHLINGSMORGEN
(SPRING MORNING)

195 NEVADA

196 PENELOPE

197 PROSPERITY

198 VANITY

199 FELICIA

200 ERFURT

201 MME ISAAC
     PÉREIRE

202 BONN

203   PINK GROOTENDORST

204   FRIEDRICH HEYER

205 KASSEL

206 NYMPHENBURG

207 PAUL'S SCARLET
CLIMBER (I)
Le Parc de la Grange, Genève

208 PAUL'S SCARLET CLIMBER (II)
Le Parc de Bagatelle, Paris

209 *ROSA MOSCHATA*

210 CHAPLIN'S PINK CLIMBER

211 CLAIR MATIN

212 DANSE DU FEU
(SPECTACULAR)

213　DANSE DES SYLPHES

214 PARADE

215 MEG

216 HAMBURGER
PHOENIX

217 MERMAID

218 PUREZZA

219 ALOHA

220 COCKTAIL

221 GOLDEN SHOWERS

222 AMERICAN PILLAR
Le Parc de Bagatelle, Paris

223 *ROSA SINO-WILSONII*

225 ZÉPHIRINE DROUHIN

226 ALBERTINE

227 MINNEHAHA

228 NEW DAWN

229   CHAPLIN'S PINK CLIMBER

230   CL. MRS PIERRE S. DU PONT

231
THE GOLDEN WALK,
CHARTWELL,
ENGLAND

232   THE QUEEN MARY ROSE GARDEN,
REGENT'S PARK, LONDON

233 LE PARC DE BAGATELLE, PARIS

ALEXANDRE GIRAULT
La Roseraie de l'Haÿ-les-Roses, Paris

235
ROSERAIE
DE L'HAŸ-LES-ROSES,
SCEAUX, PARIS

236 LE PARC DE LA GRANGE, GENÈVE

237 EL PARQUE DEL OESTE, MADRID

238
LE PARC
DE LA TÊTE D'OR,
LYON, FRANCE

239
IL ROSETO
DI ROMA

240 THE JACKSON AND PERKINS ROSE
GARDENS, NEWARK, NEW YORK

241 "OLD GARDEN ROSES"
(Mrs Temple Twining)

242 "LADY ZIA ROSES"
(Miss Julia Clements)

DESCRIPTIONS OF THE VARIETIES

Abbreviations

A.A.R.S. The All America Rose Selections; a variety which has been tried out in all the twenty-two test gardens situated in widely distributed districts of the United States, and found worthy of a special award.

A.R.S. (followed by a number). The American Rose Society rating from 1 to 10 of the garden value of a variety. 10 points indicate, in their opinion, the 'perfect' rose; 9 to 9·9 an outstanding variety; 8 to 8·9 equally excellent; 7 to 7·9 very good; 6 to 6·9 variable to good; 5 to 5·9 doubtful in some districts.

N.R.S. National Rose Society of Great Britain.

The awards indicate the outstanding qualities of the rose in that particular climate or district where it was exhibited or on trial. This is not to say that many varieties without any particular awards may not also be exceptionally good roses; many for one reason or another may not have been sent to certain trial grounds or may not have been exhibited for an award. In all cases a rose that has been introduced into commerce is no longer eligible for competition as a *new* rose for honours at any of the major exhibitions or trial grounds.

ALAIN—Floribunda (Plate 103) Meilland, 1946: ('Guinée' × 'Wilhelm') × 'Orange Triumph.' Glowing scarlet crimson, semi-double, medium size, free-flowering in large trusses, fragrant, vigorous, upright and bushy, with abundant medium green foliage; named after Alain Meilland, son of Francis Meilland, who raised it. *N.R.S. Trial Ground Certificate, 1948. Geneva Gold Medal, 1948.* A.R.S., 7·7

ALBERTINE—Climber (Plate 226) Barbier, 1921: *R. wichuraiana* × 'Mrs A. R. Waddell.' Deep salmon pink, medium size, semi-double, very free-summer-flowering, very fragrant, very vigorous for archway or pergola.

ALEXANDRE GIRAULT—Climber (Plate 234) Barbier, 1909: *R. wichuraiana* × 'Papa Gontier.' Carmine red, medium size, full, very vigorous summer-flowering, very vigorous climber, the picture shows this variety trained over a tall screen, in the gardens of La Roseraie de l'Haÿ-les-Roses, near Paris.

ALLGOLD—Floribunda (Plate 135) Le Grice, 1956: 'Goldilocks' × 'Ellinor Le Grice.'

Golden yellow, semi-double, 2½ in. across, 15 petals, fragrant, free- and perpetual-flowering, moderately vigorous, with compact bushy habit; the foliage is small, glossy deep green. Unlike so many yellow flowers, the rich yellow is kept unfadingly in all conditions of sunshine or shade. *N.R.S. Trial Ground Certificate and Gold Medal, 1956.* A.R.S., 7·5

ALOHA—Climber (Plate 219) Boerner (Jackson and Perkins), 1949: 'Mercedes Gallart' × 'New Dawn.' Rose pink, large, full, 3½ in. across, fragrant, free- and recurrent-flowering, moderately vigorous pillar rose up to 10 ft., with leathery deep green foliage.

AMA—Floribunda (Plate 113) Kordes, 1955: 'Obergärtner Wiebicke' × 'Independence.' Bright scarlet which is retained without blueing, large, 3 in. across, 25 petals, in large trusses, free-flowering, vigorous and bushy, with glossy deep green foliage.

AMERICANA—H.T. (Plate 97) Boerner (Jackson and Perkins), 1961: 'Poinsettia' seedling × 'New Yorker.'

A brilliant scarlet red, large, full, well formed, very fragrant, vigorous and strong in growth; a red variety which holds its colour without the blueing defect which appears in so many red roses as they age, on the plant or as a cut flower.

AMERICAN PILLAR—Climber (Plate 222) Van Fleet, 1902: (*R. wichuraiana* × *R. setigera*) × a red Hybrid Perpetual.
Carmine with a white eye and golden stamens, medium size, single, in large clusters on strong stems, free-summer-flowering, very vigorous as a climber 15–20 ft., or moderately vigorous when budded on a tall standard as shown in this picture.

ANGELA—Floribunda (Plate 153) Kordes, 1957: 'Masquerade' × 'Spek's Yellow.'
Golden yellow, changing to crimson and deep red as the flower matures, large, 3 in. across, full, 28 petals, free-flowering, slightly fragrant, small and large trusses, vigorous and upright, with glossy deep green foliage. *N.R.S. Trial Ground Certificate and Certificate of Merit, 1956.*

ANNA WHEATCROFT—Floribunda (Plate 124) Tantau, 1960: parentage not declared.
Light vermilion, semi-double, 3 in. across, free-flowering in small trusses, slightly fragrant, vigorous and bushy, with medium green foliage; named after the daughter of Mr and Mrs Alfred Wheatcroft of Nottingham. *N.R.S. Trial Ground Certificate, 1960.*

ANNE LETTS—H.T. (Plate 77) Letts, 1953: 'Peace' × 'Charles Gregory.'
Pale pink with paler reflex, large, full, 28 petals, fragrant, well formed, free-flowering, large deep green foliage, vigorous, and bushy; named after the mother of the raiser; a variety which needs good weather to look its best. *N.R.S. Trial Ground Certificate and Certificate of Merit, 1953.*

ASTRÉE—H.T. (Plate 48) Croix, 1955: 'Peace' × 'Blanche Mallerin.'
Rich light pink, very large, well formed, very full, free-flowering, often singly on long strong stems, very fragrant. *Lyon Gold Medal, 1955.*

AUGUST SEEBAUER—Floribunda (Plate 141) Kordes, 1944: 'Else Poulsen' × 'Break o' Day.'
Deep pink, well formed, Hybrid Tea type, full,

30 petals, 3 in. across, slightly fragrant, free-flowering, very vigorous, deep green foliage, exceptionally long-lasting as a cut flower. *N.R.S. Trial Ground Certificate, 1951.*

BABY CRIMSON—*see* PERLE D'ALCANADA (Plate 163).

BABY GOLD STAR—Miniature (Plate 162) Dot, 1940: 'Eduardo Toda' × *R. roulettii*.
Golden yellow, semi-double, slightly fragrant, height about 9 in.

BABY MASQUERADE (BABY MASKERADE)—Miniature (Plate 170) Tantau, 1956: 'Tom Thumb' × 'Masquerade.'
Yellow and red, similar to the Floribunda 'Masquerade,' but smaller, full, 25 petals, slightly fragrant, very free-flowering, compact and vigorous for its type, 10 in.

BACCARA—H.T. (Plate 19) Meilland, 1956: 'Happiness' × 'Independence.'
Brilliant deep scarlet, medium size, 72 petals, full, opening with reflexed petals, free-flowering, with deep green leathery foliage. Enormous quantities of this variety are grown under glass in the South of France and elsewhere. It is exceptionally long-lasting as a cut flower.

BAYADÈRE—H.T. (Plate 42) Mallerin, 1954: 'Mevrouw H. A. Verschuren' seedling.
Orange pink to yellow base, the outer petals veined with deeper tints, large, full, 52 petals, slightly fragrant, free-flowering, deep bronzy green foliage, vigorous and bushy. Bayadère means Indian dancing-girl, which suggests the charm of this graceful and sumptuous beauty. *N.R.S. Trial Ground Certificate and Gold Medal, 1954.*

BEAUTÉ—H.T. (Plate 41) Mallerin, 1954: 'Mme Joseph Perraud' seedling.
Yellow with a deep golden glow, slim, long-pointed, and shapely, opening to large moderately full flowers, 28 petals, fragrant, very vigorous and bushy growth, with ample deep green foliage. It should be cut young, and will then hold its graceful form till it slowly opens and its large petals flop in listless finale. *N.R.S. Trial Ground Certificate and Certificate of Merit, 1954.*

BELLE BLONDE—H.T. (Plate 80) Meilland, 1955: 'Peace' × 'Lorraine.'
Bright golden yellow, deeper in the centre, well formed, full, free-flowering, slightly fragrant, vigorous and bushy, with glossy foliage. Undoubtedly a very fine deep yellow rose, probably one of the best.

BELLE POITEVINE—Shrub, Hybrid Rugosa (Plate 189) Bruant, 1894: parentage unknown.
Magenta pink, large, semi-double, free- and recurrent-flowering, wrinkled deep green foliage, vigorous to about 3–4 ft.

BETTINA—H.T. (Plate 57) Meilland, 1953: 'Peace' × ('Mme Joseph Perraud' × 'Demain').
Orange with golden base, heavily veined, and overlaid with red and bronze, large, full, 35 petals, free-flowering, fragrant, vigorous, with olive green foliage; a fine rose for home decoration as it stands well when cut. *N.R.S. Trial Ground Certificate, 1953. Rome Certificate, 1953.*

BONN—Shrub (Plate 202) Kordes, 1950: 'Hamburg' × 'Independence.'
Orange scarlet, semi-double, large, 4 in. across, free-flowering, fragrant, very vigorous large spreading shrub or pillar rose to 9 ft. or more. *N.R.S. Trial Ground Certificate and Certificate of Merit, 1950.*

BONNIE MAID—Floribunda (Plate 137) Le Grice, 1951: parentage not declared.
Deep pink with carmine on the outside of the petals, semi-double, opening to 3 in. across, in small clusters, free-flowering, slightly fragrant, vigorous. *N.R.S. Trial Ground Certificate, 1952. Gold Medal, 1955.*

BORDER CORAL—Floribunda (Plate 151) De Ruiter, 1958: 'Signal Red' × 'Fashion.'
Coral salmon, with a tint of yellow at the base, full, medium size, 2½ in. across, free-flowering, fragrant, vigorous and spreading, with glossy deep green foliage. *N.R.S. Trial Ground Certificate and Certificate of Merit, 1957.*

BRILLIANT—H.T. (Plate 10) Kordes, 1952: 'Poinsettia' × 'Crimson Glory.'
Rich scarlet with carmine tints, very large, full, 25 petals, well formed, slightly fragrant, free-flowering, vigorous, upright, with dark green

foliage; large buds slowly opening to enormous fire red flowers shaded with deepest tints which neither blue nor burn. *N.R.S. Trial Ground Certificate, 1951. Gold Medal, 1952.* A.R.S., 6·2

BUCCANEER—H.T. (Plate 158) Swim, 1952: 'Geheimrat Duisberg' × ('Max Krause' × 'Captain Thomas').
Buttercup yellow, medium size, moderately full, 30 petals, free-flowering, fragrant, very vigorous and upright, with average height of about 5 ft.; with light pruning will make a sizeable shrub. *Geneva Gold Medal, 1952. N.R.S. Trial Ground Certificate, 1955.* A.R.S., 7·3

CARDINAL DE RICHELIEU—Shrub, Hybrid Gallica (Plate 173) Laffay, prior to 1840: parentage unknown.
Rich violet purple, small, full flowers, on a dense bush to about 4 ft. Although this hybrid is said to be of comparatively recent introduction, it is probably similar to, if not the same as, the ancient rose often mentioned by medieval chroniclers as "the Blue Rose of the Arabs."

CELSIANA—Shrub, Hybrid Damask (Plate 175), prior to 1750: parentage unknown.
A luxuriant large-leaved bush with loosely formed semi-double flowers of bright pink, strongly fragrant, to 5 ft.

CHAMPS ÉLYSÉES—H.T. (Plate 68) Meilland, 1957: 'Monique' × 'Happiness.'
Deep rich velvety crimson, flushed scarlet, medium size, full, well formed in half-open stage but opening flat, slightly fragrant, vigorous. *Madrid Gold Medal, 1957.*

CHANELLE—Floribunda (Plate 152) McGredy, 1959: 'Ma Perkins' × ('Fashion' × 'Mrs William Sprott').
Pale lemon deepening to deep saffron yellow in the centre, well formed, small Hybrid Tea type semi-double blooms, 12 petals, opening to 3 in. across, fragrant, free-flowering, vigorous and bushy, with abundant deep green foliage. *N.R.S. Certificate of Merit, 1959. Madrid Gold Medal, 1959.*

CHAPEAU DE NAPOLÉON—Shrub, Hybrid Centifolia (Plate 180) 1826: parentage unknown.
Pink, with distinct protuberant mossy winged calyx

like a cockade, the 'mossing' confined to the edges of the sepals. This habit, with some imagination, suggested the common name.

CHAPLIN'S PINK CLIMBER—Climber (Plates 210, 229) Chaplin Bros, 1928: 'Paul's Scarlet Climber' × 'American Pillar.'
Bright rich pink, with golden stamens, medium size, semi-double, large clusters, free-summer-flowering, with often a few flowers in the autumn, very vigorous climber with glossy foliage, for archway or pillar, training up bare tree-trunks, or rambling over banks or garden sheds. *N.R.S. Gold Medal, 1928.*

CHARLES DE MILLS—Shrub, Hybrid Gallica (Plate 176) prior to 1850: parentage unknown.
Full flowers of deep crimson and purple, opening flat, and then reflexing into a ball, with quartered, confused, but decorative petals; strong and vigorous growth to 5 ft.

CHARLES GREGORY—H.T. (Plate 28) Verschuren, 1947: parentage not declared.
Deep vermilion, with golden yellow on the outside of the petals, medium size, full, very fragrant, 25 petals, free-flowering, glossy deep green foliage; named after the founder of the firm of Charles Gregory and Son, Ltd, the rose nurserymen of Nottingham. *N.R.S. Trial Ground Certificate and Gold Medal, 1947.*

CHARLES MALLERIN—H.T. (Plate 60) Meilland, 1947: ('Glory of Rome' × 'Congo') × 'Tassin.'
Deep velvety scarlet crimson, with scarlet overlay towards the centre, very large, full, 40 petals, very fragrant, vigorous, and upright; named by the pupil after his master, the famous breeder of so many famous roses, who died at Varces, near Grenoble, in 1960. This rose is sometimes said to make one-sided growth, but this is frequently due to faulty pruning and cultivation. Under the best conditions it makes well-shaped free-flowering bushes with wonderful flowers that are a credit to both M. Meilland and M. Mallerin. *N.R.S. Trial Ground Certificate and Certificate of Merit, 1949. A.R.S., 6·2*

CHARLOTTE ARMSTRONG—H.T. (Plate 89) Lammerts, 1940: 'Sœur Thérèse' × 'Crimson Glory.'
Deep carmine, shaded orange and pink, large, full, 35 petals, free-flowering, slightly fragrant, vigorous and upright, with deep green foliage. It has been much used for breeding, and has produced some very fine descendants. *A.A.R.S., 1941. Portland Gold Medal, 1941. N.R.S. Trial Ground Certificate and Gold Medal, 1950. A.R.S., 9·0*

CHRISTIAN DIOR—H.T. (Plate 35) Meilland, 1959: ('Independence' × 'Happiness') × ('Peace' × 'Happiness').
Bright scarlet, large, full, perfectly formed flower, slightly fragrant, vigorous and upright growth, with ample deep green foliage; named after the world-famous *couturier. Geneva Silver-Gilt Medal, 1958. Lyon Gold Medal, 1958. Madrid Certificate, 1958. Rome Certificate, 1958. A.A.R.S., 1962.*

CHRYSLER IMPERIAL—H.T. (Plate 6) Lammerts, 1952: 'Charlotte Armstrong' × 'Mirandy.'
Vivid deep crimson, large, very full, 40 to 50 petals, well formed, very fragrant, vigorous, compact, well-shaped bush, with large deep green foliage; urn-shaped buds opening to bold well-shaped flowers, which hold their colour well; supreme among the red garden roses. *A.A.R.S., 1953. Portland Gold Medal, 1951. A.R.S., 8·8*

CINDERELLA—Miniature (Plate 162) De Vink, 1952: 'Cécile Brunner' × 'Peon.'
White tinted with carmine on the edges of the petals, very full, 35 to 40 petals, fragrant, upright, thornless, 10 in.

CIRCUS—Floribunda (Plate 105) Swim, 1955: 'Fandango' × 'Pinocchio.'
Yellow with pink and salmon shadings, deepening as the blooms age, full, 2½ in. across, 45 petals, fragrant, free-flowering, well-spaced trusses, vigorous and bushy, with deep green leathery foliage; a very fine bedding rose, which has also produced a valuable sport, found in the Wheatcroft nurseries, and named 'Alison Wheatcroft'; this is deeper and richer in colour, but otherwise similar to its parent. *N.R.S. Trial Ground Certificate and Gold Medal, 1955. Geneva Gold Medal, 1955. Rome Certificate, 1955. Bagatelle Certificate, 1955. A.A.R.S., 1956. A.R.S., 7·8*

CLAIR MATIN—Climber (Plate 211) Meilland, 1960: 'Fashion' × (('Independence' × 'Orange Triumph') × 'Phyllis Bide')).
Rich pink, medium size, single flowers, with purple stamens, free- and repeat-flowering, in clusters; a large free shrub or moderate climber up to 8 ft. *Bagatelle Gold Medal, 1960.*

CLEOPATRA—H.T. (Plate 37) Kordes, 1955: ('Walter Bentley' × 'Condesa de Sástago') × 'Spek's Yellow.'
Deep scarlet and light golden yellow, bi-colour; medium size, very full, 45 petals, borne singly on stiff stems, free-flowering, fragrant, moderately vigorous, with glossy deep green foliage. The rich colours suggested the name after the great classical Queen of Egypt. *N.R.S. Trial Ground Certificate and Gold Medal, 1955.*

CLIMBING MRS PIERRE S. DU PONT —Climber (Plate 230) Hillock, 1933: climbing sport from Mallerin's rose of the same name, which was awarded a Gold Medal at Bagatelle, in 1929.
Deep golden yellow, full, 40 petals, fragrant, very free-flowering, vigorous growth in a warm climate. This picture was taken in the Parque del Oeste, Madrid.

CLIMBING PEACE—Climber (Plate 94) 1951: sport from 'Peace.'
A vigorous climbing sport which blooms with remarkable freedom when well established, and is at its best in a warm dry climate. Mutations from 'Peace' have been introduced from several places, and some may be unreliable, so that care is necessary in choosing plants from a good source.

COCKTAIL—Climber (Plate 220) Meilland, 1957: ('Independence' × 'Orange Triumph') × 'Phyllis Bide.'
Rich crimson, shading to deep yellow in the centre, medium size, single, in clusters, large spreading shrub, or moderately vigorous pillar rose, but is at its best in a warm climate.

COCORICO—Floribunda (Plate 119) Meilland, 1950: 'Alain' × 'Orange Triumph.'
Deep warm scarlet, semi-double, 3 in. across, fragrant, strong bushy growth, with medium size deep green foliage. *N.R.S. Trial Ground Certificate*

and Gold Medal, 1951. Geneva Gold Medal, 1951. A.R.S., 8·4

COLUMBINE—Floribunda (Plate 121) Poulsen, 1956: 'Danish Gold' × 'Frensham.'
Pale yellow margined and flushed with carmine, medium size, very full, well-formed Hybrid Tea type flowers, very fragrant, flowering in clusters and on single stems, vigorous and erect. In appearance the flowers look like those of a miniature 'Peace.'

COMMONWEALTH—Floribunda (Plate 159) Kordes, 1948: 'Holstein' × 'Colonel Nicolas Meyer.'
Unfading brilliant crimson, with white centre, semi-double, 4 in. across, slightly fragrant, free- and continuous-flowering in small trusses, vigorous, with strong stems. This is one of the most outstanding Floribundas for brilliance and continuity of flower. (It must not be confused with the Hybrid Tea of the same name brought out in 1923.) *N.R.S. Trial Ground Certificate and Certificate of Merit, 1949.*

CONFIDENCE—H.T. (Plate 16) Meilland, 1951: 'Peace' × 'Michèle Meilland.'
Warm satiny pink, with yellow base, large, well formed, full, 30 petals, fragrant, deep green foliage, moderately vigorous. Photographed in the gardens of the Château de Bagatelle, this is well suited to a warm dry climate. *N.R.S. Trial Ground Certificate and Certificate of Merit, 1951. Bagatelle Gold Medal, 1951. A.R.S., 8·3*

COPPÉLIA—H.T. (Plate 34) Meilland, 1953: 'Peace' × 'Europa.'
Yellow shaded carmine, medium size, full, 28 petals, slightly fragrant, vigorous and bushy; a rose of beautiful decorative formation.

CORALIN—Miniature (Plate 171) Dot, 1955: 'Mephisto' × 'Perle d'Alcanada.'
Bright red, full, 40 petals, free-flowering, 8 in.

CRESTED MOSS—*see* CHAPEAU DE NAPOLÉON (Plate 180).

DAINTY MAID—Floribunda (Plate 138) Le Grice, 1938: 'D. T. Poulsen' seedling.
Carmine and pale pink, bi-colour, single to semi-double, free-flowering, very vigorous, for tall beds or specimen bush. *Portland Gold Medal, 1941,*

DANSE DES SYLPHES—Climber (Plate 213) Mallerin, 1960: 'Danse du Feu' × 'Toujours.'
Bright scarlet crimson, medium size, semi-double, very free-flowering in summer, and again later in autumn, in large clusters, large glossy foliage, vigorous pillar rose to 9 ft. *Madrid Certificate, 1957. Bagatelle Certificate, 1957.*

DANSE DU FEU—Climber (Plate 212) Mallerin, 1954: 'Paul's Scarlet Climber' seedling.
Bright scarlet red, medium size, full, opening flat, free- and recurrent-flowering, in clusters, moderately vigorous climber to about 10 ft. *Geneva Certificate, 1953. A.R.S., 7·6*

DEAREST—Floribunda (Plate 106) Alex. Dickson, 1960: 'Spartan' seedling.
Pale geranium lake, full, well formed, 3½ in. across, very fragrant, exceptionally so for a Floribunda, very free-flowering, vigorous and bushy, with deep green foliage. *N.R.S. Trial Ground Certificate and Certificate of Merit, 1960.*

DETROITER—*see* BRILLIANT (Plate 10).

DIAMOND JUBILEE—H.T. (Plate 24) Boerner (Jackson and Perkins), 1947: 'Maréchal Niel' × 'Feu Pernet-Ducher.'
Cream to deep buff, large, very full, 30 petals, well formed, very fragrant, free-flowering. *N.R.S. Trial Ground Certificate, 1952. A.A.R.S., 1948. A.R.S., 6·5*

DICKSON'S FLAME—Floribunda (Plate 133) Alex. Dickson, 1958: 'Independence' seedling × 'Nymph.'
Very bright pure scarlet in sunshine or rain, large, 3½ in. across, semi-double, 15 petals, in small trusses, slightly fragrant, vigorous and bushy, with deep green foliage; one of the first scarlet roses to be produced with a colour containing no trace of a mixture of blue or magenta. *N.R.S. Trial Ground Certificate, Gold Medal, and President's International Trophy, 1958.*

DR DEBAT—*see* DR F. DEBAT (Plate 53).

DR F. DEBAT—H.T. (Plate 53) Meilland, 1948: 'Peace' × 'Mrs John Laing.'
Deep warm pink shaded to gold at base, very large, 30 petals, well formed, fragrant, deep green foliage, very vigorous and upright, with strong stems.

N.R.S. Trial Ground Certificate and Gold Medal, 1950. A.R.S., 7·3

DR FAUST—*see* FAUST (Plate 120).

DOROTHY ANDERSON—H.T. (Plate 52) McGredy, 1949: 'Sam McGredy' × 'George Dickson.'
Light pink, very large, full, 33 petals, well formed, slightly fragrant, vigorous, with medium green foliage. It should be cut in the young stage as the colour begins to lose its pristine freshness as soon as it is fully open, but its perfect form, like that of its great parent, 'Sam McGredy,' holds until the petals drop. *N.R.S. Certificate of Merit, 1949.*

DUCHESS OF WINDSOR—*see* VAN NES (Plate 144).

DUCHESSE DE MONTEBELLO—Shrub, Hybrid Gallica (Plate 174) Laffay, 1842: parentage unknown.
Small round fragrant flowers of rosy pink; erect growing and compact to 5 ft.

DUET—H.T. (Plate 58) Swim, 1960: 'Fandango' × 'Roundelay.'
Rich pink on the inside of the petals and crimson on the outside, bicolour, moderately large, full, well formed, free-flowering, fragrant, vigorous and upright, with abundant leathery green foliage. *N.R.S. Trial Ground Certificate, 1960.*

EDEN ROSE—H.T. (Plate 84) Meilland, 1950: 'Peace' × 'Signora.'
Deep pink with lighter reverse, very large, full, 50 petals, well formed, globular, very fragrant, exceptionally vigorous and upright, with glossy deep green foliage. *N.R.S. Trial Ground Certificate and Gold Medal, 1950. A.R.S., 6·3*

ELSE POULSEN—Floribunda (Plate 127) Poulsen, 1924: 'Orleans Rose' × 'Red Star.'
Bright rose pink, medium size, 2½ in. across, semi-double, slightly fragrant, vigorous. The picture shows one of the large beds of roses in the Parque del Oeste, in Madrid. With 'Kirsten Poulsen,' this was one of the first Hybrid Polyanthas (subsequently called Floribundas) to be produced. It was growing in the Parque del Oeste with perfect healthy foliage, but in some districts it is sometimes rather liable to Mildew. *A.R.S., 7·6*

ENA HARKNESS—H.T. (Plate 91) Norman, 1946: 'Southport' × 'Crimson Glory.'
Bright crimson scarlet, large, full, well formed, fragrant, free-flowering, vigorous; one of the most popular red varieties, and named after the wife of W. E. Harkness, the rose nurseryman who introduced it. *N.R.S. Gold Medal, 1945. Portland Gold Medal, 1955. A.R.S., 7·0*

ERFURT—Shrub (Plate 200) Kordes, 1939: 'Eva' × 'Reveil Dijonnais.'
Bright pink shading to yellow towards the base, large, semi-double, open, 3½ in. across, fragrant, in clusters on long, strong stems, free- and recurrent-flowering, vigorous spreading bush to about 6 ft.

ESTRELLITA DE ORO—*see* BABY GOLD STAR (Plate 162).

ETHEL SANDAY—H.T. (Plate 2) Mee, 1952: 'Rex Anderson' × 'Audrey Cobden.'
Deep yellow flushed apricot, sometimes paler, large, full, 35 petals, slightly fragrant, well formed, free-flowering, deep green foliage, vigorous, upright, and bushy; not a bright colour, but a good bedding rose, and if well grown will give large specimen blooms useful for the exhibitor; named after Mrs Ethel Sanday, wife of W. J. W. Sanday, founder of the flourishing rose nursery at Bristol, England. *N.R.S. Trial Ground Certificate and Gold Medal, 1953.*

FAIRY ROSE—*see ROSA ROULETTII* (Plate 161).

FASHION—Floribunda (Plate 156) Boerner (Jackson and Perkins), 1949: 'Pinocchio' × 'Crimson Glory.'
Rich orange salmon, large, 3 in. across, full, 20 petals, free-flowering, in small and large clusters, vigorous and bushy; the first variety ever to be raised of this particularly charming colour. *N.R.S. Trial Ground Certificate and Gold Medal, 1948. Bagatelle Gold Medal and Portland Gold Medal, 1949. A.A.R.S., 1950. A.R.S., Gold Medal, 1954. A.R.S., 8·9*

FAUST—Floribunda (Plate 120) Kordes, 1956: 'Masquerade' × 'Spek's Yellow.'
Golden yellow with pink shadings, moderately full, 25 petals, large, 4 in. across when open, in very large trusses, fragrant, very vigorous, upright, and tall, with plentiful deep green foliage. *N.R.S. Trial*

Ground Certificate, Gold Medal, and President's International Trophy, 1956.

FELICIA—Hybrid Musk Shrub (Plate 199) Pemberton, 1928: 'Trier' × 'Ophelia.'
Warm pink, semi-double, fragrant, vigorous shrub to about 6 ft.

FIRECRACKER—Floribunda (Plate 114) Boerner (Jackson and Perkins), 1955: 'Pinocchio' seedling × 'Numa Fay' seedling.
Orange pink shading to deep yellow, large, semi-double, 12 to 15 petals, 4 in. across, in small trusses, very free- and perpetual-flowering, fragrant, vigorous, and bushy. *N.R.S. Trial Ground Certificate and Certificate of Merit, 1955.*

FIRST LOVE—H.T. (Plate 1) Swim, 1951: 'Charlotte Armstrong' × 'Show Girl.'
Pale pink, shaded with deeper tints, medium size, long-pointed buds, moderately full, 25 petals, fragrant, free-flowering, light green foliage, vigorous, and upright; a dainty well-shaped flower which keeps its form and is held erect on long stems for cutting; a decorative and useful variety for flower arrangements. *N.R.S. Trial Ground Certificate and Certificate of Merit, 1952. A.R.S., 8·0*

FLAMENCO—Floribunda (Plate 149) McGredy, 1960: 'Tantau's Triumph' × 'Spartan.'
Rich scarlet, lighter on the outside of the petals, large, full, opening to 3 in. across, slightly fragrant, very free-flowering, vigorous and bushy, with deep green foliage. *N.R.S. Trial Ground Certificate, 1960.*

FOR YOU—*see* POUR TOI (Plate 169).

FRED HOWARD—H.T. (Plate 65) F. H. Howard, 1950: 'Pearl Harbour' seedling.
Yellow with pink shadings, moderately large, full, 50 petals, slightly fragrant, free-flowering, very vigorous and upright, with deep green foliage; named after one of the famous rose-growers of California, U.S.A. *A.R.S., 6·6*

FRENSHAM—Floribunda (Plate 136) Norman, 1946: unnamed Floribunda seedling × 'Crimson Glory.'
Deep scarlet crimson, semi-double in large trusses, well formed, free-flowering, very vigorous and

spreading, and if lightly pruned will form a large shrub. *N.R.S. Trial Ground Certificate and Gold Medal, 1943. A.R.S. Gold Medal, 1955. A.R.S. 8·6*

FRIEDRICH HEYER—Shrub (Plate 204)
Tantau, 1956: parentage not declared.
Bright orange pink, semi-double, large, $3\frac{1}{2}$ in., free- and continuous-flowering in clusters, fragrant, deep green glossy foliage, vigorous and upright. *N.R.S. Trial Ground Certificate and Certificate of Merit, 1956.*

FRITZ THIEDEMANN—H.T. (Plate 23)
Tantau, 1961: parentage not declared.
Light scarlet vermilion, full, 36 petals, well formed, fragrant, free-flowering, vigorous and bushy, with deep green foliage; somewhat similar to 'Super Star' but a little deeper in colour; named after the famous horseman who was outstandingly successful as a rider in show jumping. *N.R.S. Trial Ground Certificate, 1960.*

FRÜHLINGSMORGEN—Shrub, Hybrid Spinosissima (Grandiflora) (Plate 194) Kordes, 1941: ('E. G. Hill' × 'Catherine Kordes') × *R. spinosissima altaica.*
Deep pink, to yellow centre, with prominent maroon stamens, single, 3 in. across, very free-flowering in May and June, and some later blooms, long arching stems to about 6 ft.

GAIL BORDEN—H.T. (Plate 25) Kordes, 1956: 'Mevrouw H. A. Verschuren' × 'Viktoria Adelheid.'
Medium rose madder, with tints of orange, to medium chrome yellow at the base, the outside of the petals similar but paler, well formed, full, large, fragrant, free-flowering, very vigorous, with deep green foliage; introduced first in America, and named by Jackson and Perkins after a prominent industrialist; a large rose of globular formation and conspicuous colour and pleasant fragrance. *N.R.S. Trial Ground Certificate and Gold Medal, 1957. A.R.S. 7·6*

GARDEN PARTY—H.T. (Plate 21) Armstrong Nurseries, 1959: 'Charlotte Armstrong' × 'Peace.'
Cream shaded pale blush pink, very large, full, rather loosely formed, 30 petals, fragrant, matt green foliage, vigorous and branching. *Bagatelle Gold Medal, 1959. A.A.R.S., 1960.*

GERTRUDE GREGORY—H.T. (Plate 47)
Gregory, 1956: sport from 'Lady Belper.'
Rich yellow, large, well formed, fragrant, free-flowering, vigorous and bushy, with deep green foliage; named after the wife of C. Walter Gregory, the rose nurseryman of Nottingham. *N.R.S. Trial Ground Certificate and Certificate of Merit, 1956.*

GIOIA—*see* PEACE (Plate 95).

GIPSY BOY—*see* ZIGEUNER KNABE (Plate 177).

GLORIA DEI—*see* PEACE (Plate 95).

GOLD CROWN—H.T. (Plate 49) Kordes, 1960: 'Peace' × 'Spek's Yellow.'
Deep rich golden yellow, very large, well formed, full, free-flowering, vigorous and upright, with deep green foliage. *N.R.S. Trial Ground Certificate, 1959. Certificate of Merit, 1960.*

GOLDEN FLEECE—Floribunda (Plate 102)
Boerner (Jackson and Perkins), 1955: 'Diamond Jubilee' × 'Yellow Sweetheart.'
Light golden yellow, large for its type, full, 35 petals, very free-flowering in small clusters, fragrant, vigorous, and bushy. *N.R.S. Trial Ground Certificate and Certificate of Merit, 1955. Bagatelle Gold Medal, 1955. A.R.S., 7·3*

GOLDEN GIANT—H.T. (Plate 61) Kordes, 1960: ('Condesa de Sástago' × 'Walter Bentley') × 'Buccaneer.'
Aureolin yellow, very full, perfectly formed, fragrant, very free-flowering, vigorous and upright, with deep green foliage. *N.R.S. Trial Ground Certificate and Gold Medal, 1960.*

GOLDEN JEWEL—Floribunda (Plate 150)
Tantau, 1960: parentage not declared.
Pale canary yellow, very full, 40 petals, 3 in. across, in open well-spaced trusses, slightly fragrant, very free-flowering, vigorous and bushy, with plentiful deep green foliage. *N.R.S. Trial Ground Certificate and Certificate of Merit, 1959.*

GOLDEN MELODY—H.T. (Plate 32) La Florida, 1934: 'Madame Butterfly' × 'Florence L. Izzard.'
Chamois yellow, frequently paler, large, well

formed, full, fragrant, vigorous; a useful decorative rose, though often cream rather than chamois.

GOLDEN SCEPTER—*see* SPEK'S YELLOW (Plate 67).

GOLDEN SHOWERS—Climber (Plate 221) Lammerts, 1956: 'Charlotte Armstrong' × 'Captain Thomas.'
Golden yellow, large, semi-double, 4 in. across, free- and recurrent-flowering, fragrant, singly and in clusters on strong stems, vigorous pillar rose to 10 ft. *A.A.R.S., 1957. Portland Gold Medal, 1957. A.R.S., 7·3*

GOLDILOCKS—Floribunda (Plate 110) Boerner (Jackson and Perkins), 1945: 'Doubloons' seedling.
Rich yellow, lighter as the flowers age, small, full, 35 petals, fragrant, free-flowering in clusters, moderately vigorous, and compact. There is a good perpetual-flowering climbing sport of this variety, with vigorous growth to about 9 ft. *N.R.S. Trial Ground Certificate and Certificate of Merit, 1948. A.R.S., 7·3*

GOLDJUWEL—*see* GOLDEN JEWEL (Plate 150).

GOLDKRONE—*see* GOLD CROWN (Plate 49).

GOLD MARIE (GOLDMARIE)—Floribunda (Plate 129) Kordes, 1958: 'Masquerade' × 'Goldenes Mainz.'
Golden yellow, deep and unfading, flushed with crimson, large, semi-double, 25 petals, with delightfully frilled edges, slightly fragrant, free-flowering in large trusses, very vigorous and upright.

GORDON EDDIE—H.T. (Plate 14) Eddie, 1949: 'Royal Visit' × 'Cynthia Brooke.'
Apricot yellow, large, full, 40 petals, fragrant, free-flowering, deep green glossy foliage, moderately vigorous and bushy. *N.R.S. Trial Ground Certificate, 1949. Gold Medal, 1950. A.R.S., 6·5*

GRACE DE MONACO—H.T. (Plate 64) Meilland, 1956: 'Peace' × 'Michèle Meilland.'
Clear rose pink, very large, globular formation, full, very fragrant, free-flowering, vigorous, and branching; named after Her Serene Highness Princess Grace of Monaco.

GRAND GALA—H.T. (Plate 62) Meilland, 1955: 'Peace' × 'Independence.'
Vivid scarlet inside the petals, silvery pink outside, bi-colour, large, full, globular formation, 50 petals, slightly fragrant, free-flowering on strong stems, vigorous, with glossy green foliage.

GRAND'MÈRE JENNY—H.T. (Plate 82) Meilland, 1950: 'Peace' × 'Signora.'
Light yellow, the outer petals and the edges flushed carmine pink, large, well formed, 30 long petals, full, slightly fragrant, free-flowering, vigorous and upright, with deep green foliage; similar colouring to that of its parent 'Peace' but with a little more of the carmine tint; also more slender in form, and not so exuberantly vigorous. *N.R.S. Trial Ground Certificate, 1949. Bagatelle Certificate, 1949. Gold Medal, 1950. Rome Gold Medal, 1955. A.R.S., 7·3*

HAMBURGER PHOENIX—Climber (Plate 216) Kordes, 1955: *R. kordesii* seedling.
Deep crimson, large, semi-double, 4 in. across, perpetual-flowering in clusters, slightly fragrant, large spreading shrub or vigorous pillar rose to 10 ft. *N.R.S. Trial Ground Certificate, 1950.*

HAWAII—H.T. (Plate 96) Boerner (Jackson and Perkins), 1960: 'Golden Masterpiece' × unnamed H.T. seedling.
Orange coral, very large, very full, fragrant, free-flowering, vigorous, with glossy medium green foliage.

HECTOR DEANE—H.T. (Plate 12) McGredy, 1938: 'McGredy's Scarlet' × 'Lesley Dudley.'
Brilliant salmon carmine, shading to yellow at the base, medium size, full, very fragrant, very vigorous; lightly pruned, will make a specimen bush. This brightly coloured decorative rose is one of the most outstandingly fragrant roses in the garden. It was named after a famous surgeon of Northern Ireland and a friend of the McGredy family. *A.R.S., 7·5*

HEIDELBERG—Shrub (Plate 192) Kordes, 1958: 'Sparrieshoop' × 'World's Fair.'
Rich crimson red, large, full, well formed, in small

and large clusters, free- and continuous-flowering, very vigorous, with dark leathery glossy foliage, about 5 ft. *N.R.S. Trial Ground Certificate and Certificate of Merit, 1958.*

HELEN TRAUBEL—H.T. (Plate 9) Swim, 1951: 'Charlotte Armstrong' × 'Glowing Sunset.'
Light warm pink, large, full, 25 petals, fragrant, vigorous, large leathery dark green foliage; a distinct and lovely luminous pink, flushed with yellow; long tapering buds opening to more loosely formed full flowers; named after Helen Traubel, the well-known soprano of the Metropolitan Opera House, New York. *N.R.S. Trial Ground Certificate, 1953. Rome Gold Medal, 1951. A.A.R.S., 1952. A.R.S., 8·7*

HERZBLUT—*see* COMMONWEALTH (Plate 159).

HOLLÄNDERIN—*see* RED FAVOURITE (Plate 111).

HUMPTY-DUMPTY—Miniature (Plate 168) De Vink, 1952: (*R. multiflora nana* × 'Mrs Pierre S. du Pont') × 'Tom Thumb.'
Shades of carmine pink, very full, 6 in.

ICEBERG—Floribunda (Plate 139) Kordes, 1958: 'Robin Hood' × 'Virgo.'
White, medium size, moderately full, 25 petals, fragrant, opening flat, well formed in the bud, 2½ in. across in trusses, free-flowering, very vigorous, with ample small light green foliage; hardly a true 'ice' colour, because there is a pink shade in the centre of the buds instead of the blue of the icebergs, but a most desirable variety whether planted singly and encouraged to grow as a small shrub, pruned to form a low hedge, or massed in a large bed as is shown in the photograph taken in the Queen Mary Rose Garden in Regent's Park, London. *N.R.S. Trial Ground Certificate and Gold Medal, 1958.*

INDEPENDENCE—Floribunda-Hybrid Tea type (Plate 98) Kordes, 1950: 'Baby Château' × 'Crimson Glory.'
Orange scarlet, moderately large, well formed, full, 35 petals, slightly fragrant, very free-flowering, vigorous and branching. This rose has had more influence on the colour of modern roses than any other since 'Soleil d'Or.' Almost all the orange-

scarlet and vermilion colouring, both in Hybrid Teas and Floribundas, is derived from this rose, and the evidence of it is nearly always shown by a distinct purplish shade on the outside at the base of the outer petals. *Bagatelle Gold Medal, 1943. N.R.S. Trial Ground Certificate and Gold Medal, 1950. A.R.S., 8·2*

IRENE CHURRUCA—*see* GOLDEN MELODY (Plate 32).

IRENE OF DENMARK—Floribunda (Plate 123) Poulsen, 1951: 'Mrs W. H. Cutbush' × 'Edina.'
White, medium size, 3 in. across, full, 40 petals, free-flowering, fragrant, moderately vigorous, and bushy. The picture shows part of a large bed in the Parque del Oeste, in Madrid. *N.R.S. Trial Ground Certificate, 1950. Certificate of Merit, 1952. A.R.S., 7·1*

IVORY FASHION—Floribunda (Plate 107) Boerner (Jackson and Perkins), 1958: 'Sonata' × 'Fashion.'
Ivory yellow to deep naples yellow, semi-double, large, 3½ in. across, 15 to 18 petals, medium size clusters, free-flowering, fragrant, vigorous and upright, with leathery medium green foliage. *N.R.S. Trial Ground Certificate and Certificate of Merit, 1957. A.A.R.S., 1959. A.R.S., 8·0*

JIMINY CRICKET—Floribunda (Plate 128) Boerner (Jackson and Perkins), 1954: 'Goldilocks' × 'Geranium Red.'
Bright salmon carmine, with orange shading, large, 2½ in. across, semi-double, 25 petals, free-flowering in well-spaced trusses, fragrant, vigorous, very bushy and spreading, small bronze green glossy foliage. *N.R.S. Trial Ground Certificate and Certificate of Merit, 1955. A.A.R.S., 1955. A.R.S., 7·6*

JOLIE MADAME—H.T. (Plate 40) Meilland, 1959: ('Independence' × 'Happiness') × 'Better Times.'
Bright light vermilion, moderately large, full, opening flat, with confused form, free-flowering, very decorative, with glossy green foliage; a brightly coloured bedding rose. *Bagatelle Certificate, 1958.*

JOSEPHINE BRUCE—H.T. (Plate 86) Bees, 1952: 'Crimson Glory' × 'Madge Whipp.'

Deep velvety crimson scarlet, large, moderately full, 24 petals, free-flowering, very fragrant, vigorous and bushy, with spreading growth, and deep green foliage. *N.R.S. Trial Ground Certificate, 1953.*

JOSEPHINE WHEATCROFT—*see* ROSINA (Plate 164).

JUNE PARK—H.T. (Plate 4) Bertram Park, 1958: 'Peace' × 'Crimson Glory.'
Rich deep pink, large well-formed blooms, often borne singly, on strong stems, full, 35 petals, very fragrant, free-flowering, large deep green foliage, vigorous spreading growth which makes it advisable to prune to upward- or inward-pointing eyes; from such aristocratic parents one would expect so worthy an offspring; richly rewarding to sight and to smell also; awarded the Clay Challenge Vase for the most fragrant rose of its year. The thick full petals may be harmed by a season of continuous wet weather, but this rose is most desirable for garden decoration and for the exhibitor; named after the well-known architect daughter of the author of this book. *N.R.S. Trial Ground Certificate and Gold Medal, 1959.*

KARL HERBST—H.T. (Plate 85) Kordes, 1950: 'Peace' × 'Independence.'
Deep red, with lighter reverse, large, well formed, very full, fragrant, very free-flowering, very vigorous, with medium green foliage; should be pruned lightly and allowance made for tall bushy growth. The flowers sometimes do not open well in the cool damp atmosphere of Northern England, but are always excellent in a somewhat drier climate. *N.R.S. Trial Ground Certificate and Gold Medal, 1950.*

KASSEL—Shrub (Plate 205) Kordes, 1957: 'Obergärtner Wiebicke' × 'Independence.'
Deep cherry red, moderately full, large, in clusters, free-flowering, fragrant, very vigorous and spreading, to 6 ft. or more. *N.R.S. Trial Ground Certificate and Certificate of Merit, 1957.*

KÄTHE DUVIGNEAU—Floribunda (Plate 155) Tantau, 1942: 'Baby Château' × *R. roxburghii* (*R. microphylla*).
Deep glowing scarlet, semi-double, opening to 3 in. across, 15 petals, in small trusses, very free-flowering, slightly fragrant, moderately vigorous

and upright, with glossy bright green foliage. *N.R.S. Trial Ground Certificate, 1952.*

KLEOPATRA—*see* CLEOPATRA (Plate 37).

KONRAD ADENAUER—H.T. (Plate 73) Tantau, 1955: 'Crimson Glory' × 'Hens Verschuren.'
Deep velvety crimson, large, full, 35 petals, free-flowering, very fragrant, globular formation, vigorous and bushy, with light green foliage; named after the Chancellor of Western Germany after the Second World War. *N.R.S. Trial Ground Certificate and Certificate of Merit, 1954. A.R.S., 7·5*

KORDES MAGENTA—*see* MAGENTA (Plate 134).

KORDES PERFECTA—*see* PERFECTA (Plate 87).

KORDES SONDERMELDUNG—*see* INDEPENDENCE (Plate 98).

KORONA—Floribunda (Plate 115) Kordes, 1954: 'Obergärtner Wiebicke' × 'Independence.'
Brilliant orange scarlet, without fading or blueing, medium to large, semi-double, 25 petals, in large clusters, slightly fragrant, very free- and continuous-flowering, vigorous, with large medium green foliage; one of the best Floribundas for massing to give a continuous show of bright colour all summer and autumn. *N.R.S. Trial Ground Certificate, 1953. Gold Medal, 1954.*

LADY BELPER—H.T. (Plate 93) Verschuren, 1948: parentage not declared.
Light orange with bronze shading, full, well formed, free-flowering, fragrant, vigorous and spreading, with deep green foliage. *N.R.S. Trial Ground Certificate and Certificate of Merit, 1948.*

LADY ELGIN—*see* THAÏS (Plate 7).

LADY SYLVIA—H.T. (Plate 90) Stevens, 1927: sport of 'Madame Butterfly.'
Light pink with yellow base, full, well formed, very fragrant, very vigorous, with long stems and few thorns; one of the most popular varieties for cut flowers, and grown in enormous quantities for the flower-markets of Great Britain.

LADY ZIA—H.T. (Plate 20) Bertram Park, 1959: 'Peace' × 'Independence.'
Rich rose red to scarlet, large, very full, very fragrant, well formed, free-flowering, with usually one bloom to a stem, vigorous growth, with beautiful deep copper-beech coloured foliage when young, maturing to olive green; is at its best in warm dry weather, and is an ideal variety for show purposes as it never loses its perfect formation. It was named after the Lady Zia Wernher, daughter of the Grand Duke Michael of Russia and wife of Sir Harold Wernher of Luton Hoo, in Bedfordshire, where is housed the fabulous Wernher Collection of works of art. *N.R.S. Trial Ground Certificate, 1958. Gold Medal, 1959.*

LA JOLLA—H.T. (Plate 26) Swim, 1954: 'Charlotte Armstrong' × 'Contrast.'
Delicate shades of pale to deep pink and yellow, well formed, moderately large, very full, 45 petals, free-flowering, fragrant, vigorous, with glossy deep green foliage; delightful as a cut flower. *N.R.S. Trial Ground Certificate, 1955.* A.R.S., 7·5

LAL—H.T. (Plate 18) Easlea, 1933: 'Commonwealth'—H.T. × 'Florence L. Izzard.'
Deep pink, lighter on the outside of the petals, full, very well formed, fragrant, free-flowering, moderately vigorous, large, deep green foliage; named after the wife of the raiser. The larger blooms often come paler or develop a pale lilac tinge with age.

LA PRESUMIDA—*see* PRESUMIDA (Plate 160).

LA ROSÉE—*see* DR F. DEBAT (Plate 53).

LEVERKUSEN—Climber (Plate 224) Kordes, 1954: *R. kordesii* × 'Golden Glow.'
Golden yellow, semi-double, large flowers, free- and recurrent-flowering sprays on long stems, vigorous pillar rose to 10 ft. Of similar growth to 'New Dawn,' it forms one of the delightful group of Kordesii Climbers which is rapidly finding favour in modern gardens instead of the non-recurrent climbing sports of the Hybrid Teas.

LILAC TIME—H.T. (Plate 3) McGredy, 1956: 'Golden Dawn' × 'Luis Brinas.'
Pale lilac, medium size, full, 30 petals, well formed,

fragrant, light green foliage, moderately vigorous. This is another step towards the blue, but it is strange that the contrasting and recessive lilac tints should have come from the parentage of a yellow rose and an orange-pink rose; one would think that it is only by development of the violet colouring that one day the true blue, for which so many hybridists are striving, will arrive. This is an inconspicuous flower in itself but can be most decorative when used as a foil for a yellow variety; in subtle combinations such as this lie the successful design and beauty of a rose garden. *N.R.S. Trial Ground Certificate and Certificate of Merit, 1955.*

LILLI MARLENE (LILLI MARLEEN)—Floribunda (Plate 126) Kordes, 1959: ('Our Princess' × 'Rudolph Timm') × 'Ama.'
Deep velvety rose red, large, 3½ in. across, semi-double, slightly fragrant, vigorous. *N.R.S. Trial Ground Certificate and Certificate of Merit, 1959.*

L'INDÉFRISABLE—*see* VAN NES (Plate 144).

LITTLE BUCKAROO—Miniature (Plate 167) Moore, 1956: (*R. wichuraiana* × 'Floradora') × ('Oakington Ruby' × 'Floradora').
Bright red, moderately full, 20 petals, fragrant, vigorous for its type, up to 14 in.

McGREDY'S YELLOW—H.T. (Plate 63) McGredy, 1933: 'Mrs Charles Lamplough' × ('Queen Alexandra Rose' × 'J. B. Clark').
Buttercup yellow, sometimes paler, large, well formed, full, 30 petals, free-flowering, slightly fragrant, vigorous, with bronze green foliage. The foliage is rather sparse so it may be planted fairly closely. It is one of the best pale yellow roses, and has remained among the leading varieties for many years, longer than do most modern roses. *N.R.S. Gold Medal, 1930.* A.R.S., 7·5

MME A. MEILLAND—*see* PEACE (Plate 95).

MME HARDY—Shrub, Hybrid Damask (Plate 179) Hardy, about 1830: parentage unknown.
White, but sometimes tinted palest pink, large, very full, cupped with typically incurved centre petals, very fragrant, vigorous, and well foliaged to 5 ft.

MME ISAAC PÉREIRE—Bourbon Shrub (Plate 201) Garçon, 1881 : parentage unknown.
Purplish crimson, large, loosely formed, free-flowering intermittently summer and autumn, fragrant, very vigorous, large spreading bush or moderate climbing rose to 10 ft.

MME KRILOFF—H.T. (Plate 50) Meilland, 1949 : 'Peace' × 'Signora.'
Orange yellow, shaded and veined deep pink, very large, full, fragrant, free-flowering, very vigorous, and bushy. *Bagatelle Gold Medal, 1944. N.R.S. Trial Ground Certificate and Gold Medal, 1948.*

MME LOUIS LAPERRIÈRE—H.T. (Plate 56) Laperrière, 1952 : 'Crimson Glory' seedling.
Rich deep crimson, moderately large, full, 40 petals, well formed, very fragrant, very free-flowering, moderately vigorous spreading growth, with ample foliage, M. Louis Laperrière named this rose after his wife. It is one of the first to open its flowers in the early summer, and every year it gains in popularity. *Bagatelle Gold Medal, 1950. N.R.S. Trial Ground Certificate and Certificate of Merit, 1952.*

MME PLANTIER—Shrub, Hybrid Alba (Plate 181) Plantier, 1835 : parentage unknown.
White, very full, in clusters, fragrant, dense, vigorous and spreading growth to about 6 ft.

MAGENTA—Floribunda (Plate 134) Kordes, 1954 : Yellow Floribunda seedling × 'Lavender Pinocchio.'
Rosy magenta to pale mauve, medium size, flowers regularly formed in rosette fashion, very free- and continuous-flowering in large trusses on long stems, very strongly fragrant, very vigorous spreading growth ; the long stems are lax, and should be lightly pruned to form well rounded bushes. It is interesting that a yellow rose, which is complementary in colour, should produce a mauve-tinted seedling.

MA PERKINS—Floribunda (Plate 122) Boerner (Jackson and Perkins), 1952 : 'Red Radiance' × 'Fashion.'
Deep pink shading to lighter tints, moderately large, 3½ in. across, moderately full, 25 petals, cup-shaped blooms in small clusters, free-flowering, fragrant, vigorous. *N.R.S. Trial Ground Certificate and Certificate of Merit, 1952. A.A.R.S., 1953. A.R.S., 7·9*

MÄRCHENLAND—Floribunda (Plate 116) Tantau, 1951 : 'Swantje' × 'Hamburg.'
Pale pink with deep pink on the outside of the petals, large, semi-double, 18 petals, fragrant, very free-flowering in large clusters, very vigorous, with deep green glossy foliage ; a good rose for hedging or as a small specimen shrub. *N.R.S. Trial Ground Certificate, 1952.*

MARGARET—H.T. (Plate 88) Alex. Dickson, 1954 : 'May Wettern' seedling × 'Souvenir de Denier van der Gon.'
Bright pink with silvery reverse, large, full, 70 petals, well formed, free-flowering, fragrant, very vigorous, with plentiful deep green foliage. The petals are soft and liable to damage in prolonged bad weather. *N.R.S. Trial Ground Certificate and Gold Medal, 1954.*

MASQUERADE (MASKERADE)—Floribunda (Plate 100) Boerner (Jackson and Perkins), 1950 : 'Goldilocks' × 'Holiday.'
Deep yellow buds, opening to pink, and gradually changing to deep red, very large trusses, very free-flowering, semi-double, 18 petals, slightly fragrant, very vigorous and bushy, with deep green foliage. Owing to the length of the flower stems there is sometimes a considerable period between the first and second flowering. *N.R.S. Trial Ground Certificate, 1951. Gold Medal, 1952. A.R.S., 7·8*

MEG—Climber (Plate 215) Gosset, 1954 : 'Paul's Lemon Pillar' × 'Madame Butterfly.'
Apricot yellow with pink shading and red stamens, semi-double, large, 4 in. across, perpetual-flowering ; a vigorous spreading pillar rose, is most effective trained as a hedge, particularly as its foliage is retained so long and in a mild winter it is almost evergreen. *N.R.S. Trial Ground Certificate and Gold Medal, 1954.*

MERMAID—Climber (Plate 217) Paul, 1917 : *R. bracteata* × a Tea Rose.
Primrose yellow with amber yellow stamens, very large single blooms, perpetual-flowering all the season until frosts ; fragrant, very vigorous, up to 30 ft. or more ; almost an evergreen, the rich deep bronzy green foliage will hold on the stems in a mild winter until the new growth of the following spring ; one of the most vigorous and truly perpetual-flowering climbing roses, or if allowed to grow as a

ree bush it will cover a large area. *N.R.S. Gold Medal, 1917.*

MESSAGE—H.T. (Plate 70) Meilland, 1956: ('Virgo' × 'Peace') × 'Virgo.'
Pure white, moderately large, well formed, full, 30 petals, fragrant, free-flowering, vigorous, and upright; where good white roses are scarce it is an excellent rose for cutting. *A.A.R.S., 1958. A.R.S., 7·2*

MEVROUW VAN STRAATEN VAN NES —*see* VAN NES (Plate 144).

MICHÈLE MEILLAND—H.T. (Plate 39) Meilland, 1945: 'Joanna Hill' × 'Peace.'
Soft salmon pink, moderately large, well formed, full, very free-flowering, slightly fragrant, vigorous; named after Michèle, the daughter of Francis Meilland. *N.R.S. Trial Ground Certificate and Certificate of Merit, 1948.*

MIDGET—Miniature (Plate 165) De Vink, 1941: 'Ellen Poulsen' × 'Tom Thumb.'
Carmine red, semi-double, 20 petals, slightly fragrant, very dwarf, 5 in.

MINNEHAHA—Climber (Plate 227) Walsh, 1905: *R. wichuraiana* × 'Paul Neyron.'
Deep rich pink, small, full, in very large clusters, very free-summer-flowering, vigorous, for pergola or archway, or weeping standard. This rambling rose has richer colouring and is more attractive than the similar variety 'Dorothy Perkins,' which is more universally grown.

MISCHIEF—H.T. (Plate 59) McGredy, 1961: 'Peace' × 'Spartan.'
Dutch vermilion inside petals, pale orange outside, full, well formed, fragrant, very free-flowering, vigorous and upright, abundant light green foliage; a variety that is noticeably continuous in its flowering, with the bushes never without colour all through the season. *N.R.S. Trial Ground Certificate and Certificate of Merit, 1960.*

MISS FRANCE—H.T. (Plate 33) Gaujard, 1955: 'Peace' × 'Independence.'
Deep vermilion, medium size, full, fragrant, opening to bright colour but confused form, free-

flowering, and vigorous, with deep green foliage; a decorative variety for massed beds in the garden. *Lyon Silver-Gilt Medal, 1955.*

MISS IRELAND—H.T. (Plate 43) McGredy, 1961: 'Tzigane' × 'Independence.'
Light dutch vermilion inside the petals, pale nasturtium orange on the outside, full, 30 petals, well formed, very free-flowering, slightly fragrant, vigorous and bushy, with deep green foliage. *N.R.S. Trial Ground Certificate and Certificate of Merit, 1960. Bagatelle Certificate, 1961.*

MRS SAM McGREDY—H.T. (Plate 27) McGredy, 1929: ('Donald McDonald' × 'Golden Emblem') × 'Queen Alexandra' seedling.
Bright orange copper to scarlet, full, 40 petals, free-flowering, fragrant, moderately vigorous, with bronze green foliage; named after the wife of the third Samuel McGredy. *N.R.S. Gold Medal, 1929. A.R.S., 7·9*

MOJAVE—H.T. (Plate 46) Swim, 1954: 'Charlotte Armstrong' × 'Signora.'
Deep orange and red flame colours, moderately large, moderately full, 25 petals, fragrant, free-flowering, vigorous tall growth, with abundant glossy foliage. The name was suggested by a description of the colouring in the Mojave Desert of America. *N.R.S. Trial Ground Certificate, 1955. A.A.R.S., 1953. Bagatelle Gold Medal, 1953. Geneva Gold Medal, 1953. A.R.S., 7·4*

MONIQUE—H.T. (Plate 29) Paolino, 1949: 'Lady Sylvia' seedling.
Silvery pink, well formed, large, full, 25 petals, very fragrant, free-flowering, very vigorous and upright, with long strong stems. *N.R.S. Trial Ground Certificate and Gold Medal, 1950.*

MONTEZUMA—H.T. (Plate 72) Swim, 1956: 'Fandango' × 'Floradora.'
Deep orange salmon, large, well formed, full, 35 petals, free-flowering, slightly fragrant, abundant deep green foliage, vigorous, and bushy; named after the Emperor of the Mexicans who so bravely tried to defend his Empire against the conquering Spaniards. *N.R.S. Trial Ground Certificate, 1955. Gold Medal, 1956. Geneva Gold Medal, 1955. Portland Gold Medal, 1957. A.R.S., 8·5*

MOULIN ROUGE—Floribunda (Plate 130) Meilland, 1952: 'Alain' × 'Orange Triumph.' Bright glowing scarlet, semi-double, 20 petals, medium size, 2½ in. across, slightly fragrant, very free-flowering, vigorous, with glossy foliage. The famous music- and dance-hall in Montmartre, Paris, suggested this name. *N.R.S. Trial Ground Certificate, Gold Medal, and President's International Trophy, 1952. Geneva Gold Medal, 1952.*

MUSK ROSE—*see ROSA MOSCHATA* (Plate 209).

NEVADA—Shrub (Plate 195) Dot, 1927: parentage recorded as 'La Geralda' × *R. moyesii*, but this has been shown to be highly improbable and almost certainly an error on the part of the raiser.
Pale creamy white, semi-double, very large, but loosely formed, free- and continuous-flowering, a vigorous graceful shrub up to about 8 ft.

NEW DAWN—Climber (Plate 228) Somerset Rose Nurseries, 1930: sport from 'Dr W. Van Fleet.'
Pale pink, semi-double, fragrant, in small and large clusters, free- and recurrent-flowering, on long stems, with ample glossy green foliage, vigorous pillar rose to 10 ft.

NYMPHENBURG—Shrub (Plate 206) Kordes, 1954: 'Sangerhausen' × 'Sunmist.'
Salmon pink with yellow base, large, semi-double, free-flowering, fragrant, vigorous, and spreading to 5 ft., with glossy foliage. *N.R.S. Trial Ground Certificate, 1954.*

OHLALA (OLALA)—Floribunda (Plate 142) Tantau, 1956: 'Fanal' seedling.
Crimson scarlet, paler towards the centre, large, semi-double, 12 petals, with golden stamens, free-flowering, in small and large clusters, very vigorous and bushy, with leathery deep green glossy foliage.

OPERA (OPÉRA)—H.T. (Plate 15) Gaujard, 1949: 'La Belle Irisée' seedling.
Bright orange red, shaded carmine, with yellow towards the base, large, well formed, fragrant, free-flowering, vigorous, leathery light green foliage. *N.R.S. Trial Ground Certificate, 1948. Gold Medal, 1949. A.R.S.,* 7·4

ORANGEADE—Floribunda (Plate 131) McGredy, 1959: 'Orange Sweetheart' × 'Independence.'
Bright deep dutch vermilion, semi-double, 3 in. across, free-flowering singly and in small trusses, slightly fragrant, vigorous; a colour which 'sings' out from all its neighbours and attracts the eye from far away. *N.R.S. Trial Ground Certificate and Gold Medal, 1959.*

PADDY McGREDY—Floribunda (Plate 118) McGredy, 1962: 'Spartan' × 'Tzigane.'
Deep coral pink, well formed, full blooms, perfectly formed, and nearly as large as a Hybrid Tea, slightly fragrant, very free-flowering, moderately vigorous, free bushy spreading habit, medium green foliage. *N.R.S. Trial Ground Certificate and Gold Medal, 1961.*

PAPILLON ROSE—Floribunda (Plate 146) Lens, 1956: 'White Briarcliff' × ('Lady Sylvia' × 'Fashion').
Rich warm pink, well formed, Hybrid Tea type flowers, full, in small clusters, fragrant, free-flowering, moderately vigorous and bushy; a delightful variety for those who look for well-shaped flowers for cutting or for button-holes, combined with the free habit of a Floribunda.

PAPRIKA—Floribunda (Plate 104) Tantau, 1958: parentage not declared.
Bright turkey red, shading a little lighter towards the centre, into which is diffused a delicate bluish tinge, semi-double, about 3½ in. across, large well-spaced clusters, very free-flowering, olive green glossy foliage, vigorous and bushy. *N.R.S. Trial Ground Certificate and Certificate of Merit, 1957. Gold Medal, 1959.*

PARADE—Climber (Plate 214) Boerner (Jackson and Perkins), 1953: 'New Dawn' seedling × 'Climbing World's Fair.'
Light crimson, large, full, but opening formless, fragrant, free- and perpetual-flowering, vigorous pillar rose to 10 ft.

PARA TI—*see* POUR TOI (Plate 169).

PARIS-MATCH—H.T. (Plate 78) Meilland, 1956: 'Independence' × 'Grand'mère Jenny.'
Warm deep pink to rose madder, large, full, well

formed, very free-flowering, large foliage, vigorous; named after the well-known Paris illustrated magazine. *Bagatelle Gold Medal, 1956.*

PAUL'S SCARLET CLIMBER—Climber (Plates 207 and 208) Paul, 1916: 'Paul's Carmine Pillar' × 'Soleil d'Or.'
Bright scarlet crimson, medium size, semi-double in small clusters, free-summer-flowering only, but occasionally gives a few autumn flowers, very vigorous pillar rose, or very decorative when budded on to tall standards; a similar variety, 'New Blaze,' gives more flowers in the autumn but does not make a spectacular specimen as does the original when trained up tall pyramids or pillars, such as may be seen at the Bagatelle gardens, in Paris, or the Parque del Oeste and other public gardens in Madrid. *N.R.S. Gold Medal, 1915. Bagatelle Gold Medal, 1918.*

PEACE—H.T. (Plate 95) Meilland, 1945: 'Souvenir de Claudius Pernet,' 'Joanna Hill,' 'Charles P. Kilham,' 'Margaret McGredy' and *R. foetida bicolor* all appear in its pedigree.
Light yellow, sometimes deep yellow, with strong shading of cerise pink towards the edges of the petals, very large, very full, 45 petals, slightly fragrant, very vigorous, with deep green leathery glossy foliage; an outstanding variety which requires light pruning for most freedom of flowering. It was in 1942 that Francis Meilland realized that he had produced a masterpiece, and named it after his mother, Mme Antoine Meilland. The occupying forces were advancing on Lyon, and in a few days he would be cut off from the rest of the world. It was essential to get the stock away to America, to his agents, the Conard-Pyle Company, of West Point, Pennsylvania. A small parcel of cuttings was entrusted to the American Consul, who, with the utmost difficulty, smuggled it out of the country. For the next three years Francis Meilland knew nothing of what had happened to his masterpiece, but Conard-Pyle had safely received the parcel of budding eyes. They had propagated them at once, and recognized the great rose that it turned out to be. It was intensively propagated, so that at the Peace Conference in San Francisco, in 1945, a bunch of the roses was ready to be placed on the table of every one of the delegates. It was named 'Peace.' Without Meilland's knowledge, during the years of the Second World War it was named 'Gioia' in Italy and 'Gloria Dei' in Germany. *Portland Gold Medal, 1944. A.A.R.S., 1946. N.R.S. Trial Ground Certificate and Gold Medal, 1947. A.R.S., 9·6*

PENELOPE—Hybrid Musk Shrub (Plate 196) Pemberton, 1924: 'Ophelia' × 'William Allen Richardson.'
Light salmon pink, medium size, semi-double, fragrant, free- and recurrent-flowering, vigorous shrub to about 5 ft. *N.R.S. Gold Medal, 1925.*

PERFECTA—H.T. (Plate 87) Kordes, 1957: 'Spek's Yellow' × 'Karl Herbst.'
A general tone of medium rose pink shading paler and then to yellow at the base, flushed with deep Rose Bengal towards the margins, paler in the autumn, very large, very full, 60 petals, very fragrant, very vigorous and free-growing, with long strong stems and ample deep green glossy foliage; an outstanding rose that is remarkably free-flowering for such a large variety, and the first flowers come usually with one flower to the stem. An outstanding variety, sometimes a little rough in the early season, and may be damaged by very bad weather, it is nevertheless one of the best Hybrid Teas for any garden and long-lasting as a cut flower. *N.R.S. Trial Ground Certificate, 1956. Gold Medal and President's International Trophy, 1957. Portland Gold Medal, 1958. A.R.S., 7·8*

PERLA DE ALCANADA—*see* PERLE D'ALCANADA (Plate 163).

PERLE D'ALCANADA—Miniature (Plate 163) Dot, 1944: 'Perle des Rouges' × *R. roulettii.* Carmine red, semi-double, very free-flowering, 10 in.

PERMANENT WAVE—*see* VAN NES (Plate 144).

PETER PAN—*see* PRESUMIDA (Plate 160).

PETITE DE HOLLANDE (PETITE JUNON DE HOLLANDE)—Shrub, Hybrid Centifolia (Plate 172), date of introduction and parentage unknown.
Very full small pink flowers freely produced on a moderately vigorous compact plant of about 4 to 4 ft. 6 in.

PICCADILLY—H.T. (Plate 44) McGredy, 1959: 'McGredy's Yellow' × 'Karl Herbst.'
Geranium lake, with overlay of vermilion, shading to buttercup yellow towards the base on the inside of the petals, pale buttercup yellow on the outside, bi-colour, large, moderately full, very free-flowering, fragrant, vigorous. *N.R.S. Trial Ground Certificate and Certificate of Merit, 1959. Rome Gold Medal, 1960. Madrid Gold Medal, 1960.*

PICTURE—H.T. (Plate 11) McGredy, 1932: parentage unknown.
Clear bright pink, medium size, full, 34 petals, well formed, slightly fragrant, free-flowering, moderately vigorous; a delicate and delightful pink rose that has lasted among the top favourites of many gardeners longer than most. *A.R.S., 8·0*

PIGALLE—H.T. (Plate 36) Meilland, 1951: 'Fantastique' × 'Paul Fromont.'
Purplish crimson with buff on the outside of the petals, and bluish shadings, very large, very full, globular, slightly fragrant, very vigorous; named after the gay and highly coloured night-club quarter of Montmartre, in Paris.

PINK GROOTENDORST—Shrub, Hybrid Rugosa (Plate 203) Grootendorst, 1923: sport from 'F. J. Grootendorst.'
Rose pink, small, full, fringed petals, in large clusters, free- and continuous-flowering, vigorous to about 4 ft., small crinkled foliage.

PINK PEACE—H.T. (Plate 13) Meilland, 1959: ('Peace' × 'Monique') × ('Peace' × 'Mrs John Laing').
Rich rose pink to carmine, large, perfectly formed, very fragrant, vigorous; strong bushy plant with clear green foliage. This is a seedling from 'Peace' but is much more restrained in its vigorous growth than its parent. *Madrid Certificate, 1959. Bagatelle Certificate, 1959. Rome Gold Medal, 1959. Geneva Gold Medal, 1959. Lyon Certificate, 1959. A.R.S., 7·3*

PINOCCHIO—Floribunda (Plate 148) Kordes, 1940: 'Eva' × 'Geheimrat Duisberg.'
Warm pink, small, rosette-shaped, very full, 30 petals, free-flowering in large trusses, fragrant, vigorous, and bushy. *Portland Gold Medal, 1942. N.R.S. Trial Ground Certificate and Certificate of Merit, 1949. A.R.S., 7·8*

POLY PRIM—Floribunda (Plate 125) Eddie, 1954: 'Goldilocks' × 'Geheimrat Duisberg.'
Deep yellow, shading paler as it opens, very full, 60 petals, 3 in. across, free-flowering in small clusters, fragrant, moderately vigorous and bushy. *N.R.S. Trial Ground Certificate and Gold Medal, 1954.*

POMPON DE PARIS—*see ROSA ROULET-TII* (Plate 161).

POUR TOI—Miniature (Plate 169) Dot, 1946: 'Eduardo Toda' × *R. roulettii*.
White tinted yellow at the base, semi-double, 8 in.

PRELUDE—H.T. (Plate 51) Meilland, 1955: 'Fantastique' × ('Ampère' × ('Charles P. Kilham' × 'Capucine Chambard')).
Pale lavender mauve, medium size, moderately full, 25 petals, moderately vigorous; one of the first Hybrid Tea type roses to be introduced of a lavender mauve shade, inclining a step towards that mirage of the rose breeder—a blue rose.

PREMIER BAL (improved)—H.T. (Plate 76) Meilland, 1955: ('Fantastique' × 'Caprice') × 'Peace.'
White shading to deep carmine pink on the edges of the petals, full, 45 petals, free-flowering, very fragrant, vigorous, and bushy. This variety replaces and supersedes the variety of the same name introduced in 1950; a rose which is only at its best in fine warm weather, but at its best is superb in its colour; a most beautiful rose for those who can grow it in the right climate.

PRESIDENT HERBERT HOOVER—H.T. (Plate 75) Coddington, 1930: 'Sensation' × 'Souvenir de Claudius Pernet.'
Red to orange and deep pink, moderately large, full, 25 petals, fragrant, very vigorous and upright, with rather sparse foliage; a good rose for cutting with long stems. *A.R.S., 7·7*

PRESUMIDA—Miniature (Plate 160) Dot, 1948: 'Eduardo Toda' × *R. roulettii*.
Pale yellow to white with deep yellow centre, 10 in.

PROSPERITY—Hybrid Musk Shrub (Plate 197) Pemberton, 1919: 'Marie-Jeanne' × 'Perle des Jardins.'
White, sometimes tinted pink, full medium size,

opening flat in large clusters, vigorous spreading shrub or moderate climber, about 6 ft.

PUREZZA—Climber, Hybrid Banksiae (Plate 218) Mansuino, 1961: parentage not declared.
White, small, full, very free- and continuous-flowering, very vigorous climber, for pillar or pergola. There are two varieties with similar but reversed parentage which, with similar and equally attractive flowers, have remained dwarf miniature plants of only a few inches in growth. *Rome Gold Medal, 1960.*

QUEEN ELIZABETH—Floribunda (Plate 99) Lammerts, 1955: 'Charlotte Armstrong' × 'Floradora.'
Clear self pink, medium size flowers, borne singly and in small clusters, full, 25 petals, free-flowering, fragrant, long—almost thornless—stems, abundant deep green leathery foliage, very vigorous; good for massing, and for hedges if the stems are pruned at different heights to keep the lower parts well clothed. This is a picture from the Queen Mary Rose Garden in Regent's Park, London. Permission was given to the raiser, Mr Lammerts, to name the rose after Queen Elizabeth II by the British Consul in San Francisco, after he had communicated with Government offices in London. Her Majesty graciously accepted a large bed of it, presented by the National Rose Society, which was planted in the gardens of Buckingham Palace. *N.R.S. Trial Ground Certificate, Gold Medal, and the President's International Trophy awarded for the best new rose of its year, 1955. A.A.R.S., 1955. A.R.S., 9·0*

RED FAVOURITE—Floribunda (Plate 111) Tantau, 1951: 'Karl Weinhausen' × 'Cinnabar.'
Deep crimson scarlet, semi-double, medium size, 25 petals, 2½ in. across, slightly fragrant, free-flowering, in large clusters, moderately vigorous. *N.R.S. Trial Ground Certificate and Certificate of Merit, 1952. A.R.S., 7·5*

RED WONDER—Floribunda (Plate 147) De Ruiter, 1954: 'Better Times' seedling.
Scarlet crimson, large, 3½ in. across, full, 25 petals, in small trusses, free-flowering, fragrant, vigorous and bushy, with glossy leathery foliage. *N.R.S. Trial Ground Certificate, 1954. A.R.S., 7·6*

REINA ELISENDA—*see* INDEPENDENCE (Plate 98).

ROSA CENTIFOLIA CRISTATA—*see* CHAPEAU DE NAPOLÉON (Plate 180).

ROSA CHINENSIS MINIMA—*see* *ROSA ROULETTII* (Plate 161).

ROSA GALLICA VERSICOLOR—*see* *ROSA MUNDI* (Plate 178).

ROSA MOSCHATA—Climber (Plate 209) known since the Middle Ages.
From the Middle East to Central Asia and the Himalayas; white, small, single, fragrant, very free-summer-flowering, followed by small red heps in the autumn; an enormously vigorous climber which in a warm climate will ramble without restraint over shrubs and trees up to 40 or 50 ft. This Musk Rose has never been known naturalized in Great Britain so could not be the Musk Rose of Shakespeare. The Musk Rose of *A Midsummer Night's Dream* was probably *R. arvensis*, the 'field' rose of the English countryside.

ROSA MOYESII—Shrub (Plate 185) introduced into Europe 1894.
From Western China; deep blood red single flowers, followed by very large bottle-shaped red heps in the autumn; a very vigorous, slender, and tall-growing shrub to 10 ft.

ROSA MUNDI—Shrub, Hybrid Gallica (Plate 178) known since the fifth century: sport of *R. gallica officinalis.*
Light crimson, heavily striped and splashed with pink and white, and sometimes all crimson, vigorous bush to 4 ft.; associated by some early chroniclers with "Fair Rosamond," Rosamond Clifford, mistress of Henry II, whose tomb at Godstow Abbey (now a ruin), near Oxford, was of beaten brass, and bore the inscription:

Hic jacet in tumba Rosa mundi, non Rosa munda;
Non redolet, sed olet, que redolere solet.

"Here Rose the graced, not Rose the chaste, reposes;
The smell that rises is no smell of roses."

ROSA ODORATA MAJOR—Shrub (Plate 193) introduced into Europe in the nineteenth century.
Chinese garden rose; pale pink, full, about 2½ in. across, very free- but summer-flowering only,

vigorous bushy shrub or moderate climber, a variety which is used for making understocks, propagated from cuttings, for glasshouse roses. In the hot drier climate of the Mediterranean area it is extensively used for this purpose.

ROSA OMEIENSIS PTERACANTHA—Shrub (Plate 182) introduced into Europe in the nineteenth century.
From Western China; immense quantities of small, 4-petalled white flowers in early summer; brown stems, armed with enormous broad thorns, translucent ruby red when young, very hard and sharp when mature; a vigorous impenetrable shrub to 15 ft. tall and as much wide. It may be hard pruned to obtain long young flowerless shoots for decorative purposes.

ROSA PRIMULA—Shrub (Plate 184) collected in Turkestan and Northern China about 1890.
Primrose yellow, very free early summer-flowering, on brown prickly stems, very fragrant, myrrh scented foliage, 6 to 7 ft. In favourable conditions it will spread by underground suckers into a very large thicket and considerably taller. The fragrant foliage, on a warm moist summer evening, will scent the air for many yards around.

ROSA ROULETTII—Miniature (Plate 161) introduced into Europe in the early nineteenth century.
Rose red, fine foliage of typical Chinensis pattern, very free-flowering, up to 8 in. on its own roots, but taller if grafted.

ROSA RUGOSA SCABROSA—Shrub (Plate 190) introduced into Europe in the nineteenth century.
From Japan; deep purplish pink, very large single flowers, 5 in. across, free- and continuous-flowering, each flower followed by a very large red hep like a small tomato; dense vigorous bush to about 6 ft., very spiny stems and middle green wrinkled foliage. There is a white variety which is similar but has rather smaller flowers, also a double white variety named 'Blanc Double de Coubert' which again is similar in habit with the exception of its loosely formed double white flowers.

ROSA SERICEA PTERACANTHA—see *ROSA OMEIENSIS PTERACANTHA* (Plate 182).

ROSA SINO-WILSONII—Climber (Plate 223) introduced into Europe at the beginning of the twentieth century.
From China; white, single, small, with bright yellow stamens, very free-flowering, in enormous clusters, in June, and July, with very decorative bright orange yellow heps in the autumn which persist on the branches right through to the spring, very vigorous climbing rose which will ramble freely over trees and shrubs up to 20 ft. or more.

ROSA SPINOSISSIMA ALTAICA—Shrub (Plate 186) introduced into Europe at the beginning of the nineteenth century.
From the Altai Mountains of Siberia; creamy white, large single flowers, a vigorous shrub to 5 or 6 ft. Accustomed to the rigorous climate of its ancestors, it is one of the earliest to flower when brought to milder conditions, and heralds the coming of the rose season. The name Grandiflora has been borrowed and misused to describe certain roses of American origin.

ROSA WILLMOTTIAE—Shrub (Plate 183) introduced into Europe at the beginning of the twentieth century.
From Western China; small rosy red flowers, on short lateral branchlets, decorative fernlike foliage of light glaucous green; numerous small red heps in the autumn; spreading prickly shrub to 10 ft. tall and as much broad.

ROSE GAUJARD—H.T. (Plate 45) Gaujard, 1958: 'Peace' × 'Opera' seedling.
White flushed with pale pink, shading and veining strongly to deep rose towards the margins, large, well formed, full, free-flowering, often singly on long strong stems, fragrant, very vigorous, with deep green glossy foliage. M. Jean Gaujard had such faith in this rose that he named it after himself. *Lyon Gold Medal, 1957. N.R.S. Trial Ground Certificate, 1957. Gold Medal, 1958.*

ROSEMARY ROSE—Floribunda (Plate 101) De Ruiter, 1954: 'Gruss an Teplitz' × a Floribunda seedling.
Bright carmine, regularly formed like a camellia, full, fragrant, vigorous, with attractive foliage, reddish bronze when young; named after Rosemary, the daughter of C. Walter Gregory, who introduced the rose to British gardeners. *N.R.S.*

Trial Ground Certificate and Gold Medal, 1954. Rome Gold Medal, 1954.

ROSENMÄRCHEN—*see* PINOCCHIO (Plate 148).

ROSERAIE DE L'HAŸ—Shrub, Hybrid Rugosa (Plate 191) Cochet-Cochet, 1901 : reported to be a sport from *R. rugosa rosea.*
Purplish crimson, large, full, very fragrant, loosely formed, free- and continuous-flowering to 7 ft.; a very decorative, well balanced, tall and spreading plant for the shrub garden.

ROSE VAN SIAN—*see* CARDINAL DE RICHELIEU (Plate 173).

ROSINA—Miniature (Plate 164) Dot, 1951: 'Eduardo Toda' × *R. roulettii.*
Buttercup yellow, semi-double, 16 petals, slightly fragrant, free-flowering, vigorous for its type; up to 16 in.

RUBAIYAT—H.T. (Plate 17) McGredy, 1949: ('McGredy's Scarlet' × 'Mrs Sam McGredy') × 'Sir Basil McFarland' seedling.
Rich rose carmine, large, well formed, full, 25 petals, free-flowering, very vigorous. *Portland Gold Medal, 1945. A.A.R.S., 1947. A.R.S., 8·2*

RUMBA—Floribunda (Plate 140) Poulsen, 1960: ('Poulsen's Bedder' × 'Floradora') × 'Masquerade.'
Lemon yellow changing on the edges of the petals to deep orient red and dutch vermilion, small, opening to 2 in. across, full, 38 petals, very free-intermittent-flowering, fragrant, bushy growth, with abundant deep green foliage. *N.R.S. Trial Ground Certificate and Certificate of Merit, 1959.*

SABRINA—H.T. (Plate 79) Meilland, 1960: 'Grand Gala' × 'Premier Bal.'
Crimson inside the petals, pale orange and carmine on the outside, large, very full, globular formation, fragrant, very vigorous and bushy, strong stems and deep green foliage. *N.R.S. Trial Ground Certificate and Certificate of Merit, 1960.*

SARABANDE—Floribunda (Plate 108) Meilland, 1957: 'Cocorico' × 'Moulin Rouge.'
Bright dazzling scarlet, semi-double, 3½ in. across, very free- and continuous-flowering, in large trusses, slightly fragrant, moderately vigorous spreading growth. *Bagatelle Gold Medal, 1957. Geneva Gold Medal, 1957. Rome Certificate, 1957. Madrid Gold Medal, 1957. Lyon Certificate, 1957.*

SARAH VAN FLEET—Shrub, Hybrid Rugosa (Plate 187) Van Fleet, 1926: parentage unknown.
Bright rose pink, large, semi-double, free- and continuous-flowering, very fragrant, 6 ft.

SCHLÖSSERS BRILLANT—*see* BRILLIANT (Plate 10).

SCHNEEWITTCHEN—*see* ICEBERG (Plate 139).

SCHNEEZWERG—Shrub, Hybrid Rugosa (Plate 188) Lambert, 1912: probably *R. rugosa* × a white Hybrid Polyantha.
Snow white, small, semi-double, opening flat with golden stamens, continuous-flowering, with scarlet heps concurrently, prickly bush to about 5 ft.

SCHWEIZER GRUSS — *see* RED FAVOURITE (Plate 111).

SHEPHERD'S DELIGHT—Floribunda (Plate 154) Alex. Dickson, 1958: 'Masquerade' seedling × 'Joanna Hill.'
Dutch vermilion shading to indian yellow in centre; large, 3 in. across, semi-double, 15 petals, slightly fragrant, large and small well-spaced clusters, very vigorous, with matt deep green foliage; lightly pruned will make a medium-size shrub. *N.R.S. Trial Ground Certificate and Certificate of Merit, 1957.*

SHOW GIRL—H.T. (Plate 31) Lammerts, 1949: 'Joanna Hill' × 'Crimson Glory.'
Deep carmine pink, very large, well formed, full, 20 petals, fragrant, long stems, very vigorous. *N.R.S. Trial Ground Certificate, 1949. Gold Medal, 1950. A.R.S., 7·6*

SILVER LINING—H.T. (Plate 81) Alex. Dickson, 1959: 'Karl Herbst' × 'Eden Rose' seedling.
Silvery rose, large, full, 30 petals, free-flowering, fragrant, vigorous, with deep green foliage. A large bed of this was graciously accepted by Queen Elizabeth II for the grounds of Buckingham Palace. *N.R.S. Trial Ground Certificate and Certificate of Merit, 1957. Gold Medal, 1958.*

SNOW DWARF—*see* SCHNEEZWERG (Plate 188).

SORAYA—H.T. (Plate 38) Meilland, 1956: ('Peace' × 'Floradora') × 'Grand'mère Jenny.'
Brilliant orange red with deeper shadings, large, full, 30 petals, free-flowering, slightly fragrant, long strong stems, vigorous; named after Soraya, one-time Queen of Persia. *Lyon Gold Medal, 1955.*

SOUVENIR DE JACQUES VERSCHUREN —H.T. (Plate 54) Verschuren-Pechtold, 1950: 'Katharine Pechtold' × 'Orange Delight.'
Deep orange salmon, medium size, full, moderately fragrant, free-flowering, vigorous, and upright. *N.R.S. Trial Ground Certificate, 1950. Certificate of Merit, 1951.*

SPARTAN—Floribunda (Plate 157) Boerner (Jackson and Perkins), 1954: 'Geranium Red' × 'Fashion.'
Rich salmon to light red, very full, 3 in. across, well formed, 30 petals, very fragrant, very free-flowering, vigorous, and bushy; a variety that is being extensively used in hybridizing in the search for flowers of Hybrid Tea type on bushes of Floribunda type growth. *N.R.S. Trial Ground Certificate, Gold Medal and President's International Trophy, 1954. Portland Gold Medal, 1955. A.R.S., 8·3*

SPECTACULAR—*see* DANSE DU FEU (Plate 212).

SPEK'S YELLOW—H.T. (Plate 67) Verschuren-Pechtold, 1947: 'Golden Rapture' seedling.
Bright rich yellow, moderately large, well formed, full, 35 petals, slightly fragrant, free-flowering in large trusses, vigorous and tall; holds its colour well without fading. *N.R.S. Trial Ground Certificate, 1947. A.R.S., 7·3*

SPRING MORNING—*see* FRÜHLINGS-MORGEN (Plate 194).

STELLA—H.T. (Plate 66) Tantau, 1959: parentage not declared.
The outer petals have carmine on the margins, shading to almost white in the centre, the inner petals similar but paler, very large, very full, well formed, fragrant, vigorous. *N.R.S. Trial Ground Certificate, 1959. Gold Medal, 1960.*

SUPER STAR—H.T. (Plate 8) Tantau, 1960: 'Peace' seedling × 'Alpine Glow' ('Alpenglühen') seedling.
Light vermilion, moderately large, perfectly formed, full, 33 petals, very free-flowering, fragrant, tough, glossy, deep green foliage, very vigorous, tall, and bushy; a sensational and completely new colour such as sometimes, but at long intervals, breaks upon the World of Roses; a pure light vermilion tint hitherto unknown among Hybrid Tea type roses. *N.R.S. Trial Ground Certificate, Gold Medal, and the President's International Trophy for the best new rose of the year, Geneva Gold Medal, Madrid Certificate, 1960.*

SUSPENSE—H.T. (Plate 22) Meilland, 1960: 'Henri Mallerin' × ('Happiness' and 'Floradora').
Rich deep scarlet, with orange reverse, very large, free-flowering, slightly fragrant, very vigorous, tall branching plants, with ample rich green foliage; the flowers open wide to a huge size with confused form in the petals but brilliant as a garden plant. *Lyon Gold Medal, 1960.*

SUTTER'S GOLD—H.T. (Plate 71) Swim, 1950: 'Charlotte Armstrong' × 'Signora.'
Golden orange, shaded indian red in the young flower but lighter as it expands, moderately large, well formed, full, 35 petals, very fragrant, very vigorous, and upright. *Portland Gold Medal, 1946. Bagatelle Gold Medal, 1948. Geneva Gold Medal, 1949. A.A.R.S., 1950. N.R.S. Trial Ground Certificate, 1950. Certificate of Merit, 1951. A.R.S., 8·1*

SWEET REPOSE—Floribunda (Plate 109) De Ruiter, 1955: 'Geheimrat Duisberg' × a Polyantha.
Light yellow and pink to deep pink, full, 25 petals, 3 in. across, very free-flowering, fragrant, in large clusters, vigorous, with deep green foliage; a photograph taken in the Queen Mary Rose Garden in Regent's Park, London. *N.R.S. Trial Ground Certificate and Gold Medal, 1955.*

SYMPHONIE—H.T. (Plate 69) Meilland, 1951: 'Peace' × ('Signora' × 'Mrs John Laing').
Deep pink, strongly veined, and shaded carmine, well formed, very large, full, 25 petals, free-flowering, very fragrant, light green foliage, vigorous, and bushy. *N.R.S. Trial Ground Certificate and Gold Medal, 1949. A.R.S., 7·1*

TALLYHO—H.T. (Plate 30) Swim, 1949: 'Charlotte Armstrong' seedling.

Carmine to red, large, well formed, full, 35 petals, very fragrant, very vigorous, and upright. *N.R.S. Trial Ground Certificate, 1949. A.A.R.S., 1949. A.R.S., 8·4*

THAÏS—H.T. (Plate 7) Meilland, 1954: 'Mme Kriloff' × ('Peace' × 'Genève').
Orange yellow flushed with pink, large, full, 35 petals, fragrant, free-flowering, long stems, deep leathery green foliage, vigorous, upright, and bushy—a picture made in the beautiful garden of the Parque del Oeste, Madrid. *A.R.S., 7·6*

THE OPTIMIST—*see* SWEET REPOSE (Plate 109).

THE PEOPLE—Floribunda (Plate 132) Tantau, 1954: 'Tantau's Triumph' × ('Käthe Duvigneau' × 'Tantau's Triumph').
Bright orange scarlet, large, 3½ in. across, in small trusses, full, 26 petals, free-flowering, slightly fragrant, vigorous, and bushy. *N.R.S. Trial Ground Certificate, 1954. Gold Medal, 1955.*

TIFFANY—H.T. (Plate 74) Lindquist, 1954: 'Charlotte Armstrong' × 'Girona.'
Rich salmon pink, shading to golden yellow at the base, large, full, well formed, 30 petals, very fragrant, free-flowering on long stems, very vigorous, with deep green foliage. *A.A.R.S., 1955. A.R.S., 8·8*

TINKER BELL—Miniature (Plate 166) De Vink, 1954: 'Ellen Poulsen' × 'Tom Thumb.'
Bright rose pink, full, 45 petals, free-flowering, bushy, 8 in.

TITANIA—*see* PERLE D'ALCANADA (Plate 163).

TIVOLI—Floribunda (Plate 145) Poulsen, 1955: 'Poulsen's Supreme' × ('Souvenir de Claudius Denoyel' × 'Hvissinge-Rose').
Warm pink, with yellow to the centre, 3 in. across, full, 24 petals, in clusters, free-flowering, fragrant, very vigorous, with glossy deep green foliage. *N.R.S. Trial Ground Certificate and Certificate of Merit, 1954.*

TOISON D'OR—*see* GOLDEN FLEECE (Plate 102).

TROPICANA—*see* SUPER STAR (Plate 8).

TZIGANE—H.T. (Plate 55) Meilland, 1951: 'Peace' × 'J. B. Meilland.'

Bright scarlet red inside and chrome yellow on the outside of the petals, bi-colour, moderately large, well formed, full, fragrant, free-flowering, glossy copper-beech coloured foliage, vigorous and upright; a popular and brightly coloured bedding rose which, owing to unlucky circumstances, seems to have been overlooked when competing for the highest honours. 'Tzigane' is like a "sunburnt gipsy girl." *A.R.S., 7·4*

VANITY—Hybrid Musk Shrub (Plate 198) Pemberton, 1920: 'Château de Clos Vougeot' seedling.
Rose pink, semi-double, free-flowering, in large sprays, very fragrant, leathery rich green foliage, very vigorous, up to about 10 ft.

VAN NES—Floribunda (Plate 144) Leenders, 1934: sport from 'Else Poulsen.'
Deep carmine, large, semi-double, with frilled edges, small and large clusters, free-flowering, vigorous and upright, with copper-beech coloured foliage. *Bagatelle Gold Medal, 1933.*

VIRGO—H.T. (Plate 83) Mallerin, 1947: 'Blanche Mallerin' × 'Neige Parfum.'
White sometimes flushed pale pink, medium size, well formed, moderately full, 30 petals, slightly fragrant, very free-flowering, vigorous, with small foliage; a very good variety for cutting with long stems and few thorns. *N.R.S. Trial Ground Certificate and Gold Medal, 1949.*

VOGUE—Floribunda (Plate 112) Boerner (Jackson and Perkins), 1949: 'Pinocchio' × 'Crimson Glory.'
Soft deep pink, moderately large, well formed, 4 in. across, full, 25 petals, very free-flowering, very fragrant, vigorous and bushy, with glossy medium green foliage; a sister seedling, actually from the same seed-pod as the very popular 'Fashion.' *N.R.S. Trial Ground Certificate, 1950. Certificate of Merit, 1951. Portland Gold Medal, 1950. Geneva Gold Medal, 1950. A.A.R.S., 1952. Bagatelle Certificate, 1950. A.R.S., 8·2*

WENDY—*see* POUR TOI (Plate 169).

WENDY CUSSONS—H.T. (Plate 92) Gregory, 1959: 'Independence' × 'Eden Rose.'
Deep rose red paler on the outside, full, 37 petals, well formed, free-flowering, very fragrant, vigorous, and branching, with deep green glossy foliage.

N.R.S. Trial Ground Certificate, Gold Medal, and President's International Trophy, 1959. First Certificate Rome, 1960.

WHITE KNIGHT—*see* MESSAGE (Plate 70).

WHITE SWAN—H.T. (Plate 5) Verschuren-Pechtold, 1951 : 'Kaiserin Auguste Viktoria' seedling.
Pure white, large flowers, full, 30 petals, very well formed, fragrant, free-flowering, glossy dark green foliage, very vigorous and upright; one of the best and most regularly shaped white roses, and exceptionally long-lasting as a cut flower. *A.R.S.,* 6·9

YELLOWHAMMER—Floribunda (Plate 143) McGredy, 1954: 'Poulsen's Yellow' seedling.
Rich unfading golden yellow, semi-double, $2\frac{1}{2}$ in. across, in small trusses, free-intermittent-flowering, slightly fragrant, moderately vigorous, bushy. *N.R.S. Trial Ground Certificate and Gold Medal, 1954.*

ZAMBRA—Floribunda (Plate 117) Meilland, 1961 : ('Goldilocks' × 'Fashion') (A) × ('Goldilocks' × 'Fashion') (B).
Bright orange, semi-double, very free-flowering, moderately vigorous and bushy, with medium green glossy foliage. *N.R.S. Trial Ground Certificate, 1961. Rome Gold Medal, 1961. Bagatelle Gold Medal, 1961.*

ZÉPHIRINE DROUHIN—Bourbon Climber (Plate 225) Bizot, 1868: parentage unknown.
Clear rose pink, large, semi-double, free- and continuous-flowering, very fragrant, moderate climber, with almost thornless stems; may also be grown as a large free shrub or trained as a hedge.

ZIGEUNER KNABE—Bourbon Shrub (Plate 177) Lambert, 1909: parentage not declared.
Deep crimson purple, medium size, opening flat but with regular formation, fragrant, free-summer-flowering but not perpetual, vigorous to 5 ft.; the most recent, and probably the last, which will be added to the Bourbon group of roses.

SOME FAMOUS ROSE GARDENS

GOLDEN WALK, CHARTWELL, ENGLAND (Plate 231).
The Golden Walk at Chartwell, England, the home of Sir Winston and Lady Churchill, was planted in 1958, as a gift from their family to celebrate the golden wedding of the great statesman and his wife. There are fifty Standards (Tree Roses) in twenty-eight different varieties, and about three hundred bushes, in this unique rosary. These roses are all depicted full-scale in water-colour by famous artists, and the pictures are beautifully bound in a book which was part of this family celebration.

JACKSON AND PERKINS ROSE GARDENS, NEWARK, NEW YORK (Plate 240).
The seventeen-acre rose garden that the Jackson and Perkins Company maintains for the public, in Newark, New York, U.S.A., has brought national and international fame to a town whose population barely exceeds ten thousand persons. Each year more than 500,000 visitors come to see the spectacular display provided by millions of blossoms produced by more than thirty-six thousand rose-plants. Every important variety available to rose-growers to-day may be seen here either in the formal, mass plantings or in small, informal gardens. Climatic conditions in Newark are at their best for rose-growing—situated in the rolling foothills at the head of New York's Finger Lake region, Newark is cooled in the summer by fresh winds from Canada and in the winter it is covered by a protective blanket of snow. Every type of rose, including Hybrid Teas, Floribundas, Miniatures, Climbers, and Standards (Tree Roses), plus a wide variety of colourful perennials, may be seen here. From June until the first killing frosts in the autumn, the garden is open to the public free of charge.

PARC DE BAGATELLE, PARIS (Plate 233).
The history of the charming little Château de Bagatelle is long and vastly entertaining, but that which interests us most at the moment dates from 1907, when the house, park, and gardens were acquired by the City of Paris and the gardens newly laid out by Forestier. The present rose garden is therefore of recent foundation but has already become famous throughout the world, particularly for its international 'Concours' for new varieties of roses held annually. Here raisers of new

roses send their productions, five plants of H.T.'s and Floribunda or two plants of Climbers. They are under trial for two years (three for Climbers), during which exact records are kept of their behaviour, number of flowers produced, and other details. In June an international jury meets and, with the records before it, awards points to the second-year plants under the various headings to select finally the Rose of the Year for the Bagatelle Gold Medal and the special certificates.

PARC DE LA GRANGE, GENÈVE (Plate 236).

This most decorative garden overlooking Lac Léman, or Lake of Geneva, is embellished with the architectural features of a tall pergola, or pavilion, flowing fountains, and beautiful statuary. It is maintained by the City of Geneva, and is the scene of frequent festivals, when the flower-beds are individually and brilliantly illuminated by permanently installed flood-lighting. Hybridists from all over the world send their productions here for testing and trial, and an annual 'Concours' is held when an international jury awards the Gold Medal and other valuable prizes to the outstanding varieties.

PARC DE LA TÊTE D'OR, LYON, FRANCE (Plate 238).

Lyon may be said to be the birthplace of the modern rose, for it was near here, in the early years of the present century, that Pernet-Ducher produced the first yellow roses. The architecturally designed rose garden is comparatively small, and is the centre of an annual 'Concours' for new varieties of roses, which are confined to the productions of French raisers. The winning variety is named as "La plus belle Rose de France."

PARQUE DEL OESTE, MADRID (Plate 237).

This famous garden is often called, and with justice, the most beautiful rose garden in the world. In 1954, on what was originally a veritable rubbish dump on a steep slope below the Royal Palace, it was created by importing enormous quantities of the richest agricultural soil to level some eight acres. On the east, with a background of the tree-planted hillside, are the pavilions, some beautiful statuary, and fountains. To either side is extended a great semicircle of iron-framed pergola clothed with climbing roses. Thus partly enclosed are the geometrically designed beds of some three hundred varieties in beds of sixty to a hundred of each variety, each bed with its installed flood-lighting for illuminations at night-time. With adequate watering, careful and continuous cultivation, the conditions are set for a display of roses which cannot be found elsewhere in such perfection. An annual 'Concurso' is held here for new varieties of roses which are submitted from growers all over the world, and valuable prizes are awarded by an international jury to the outstanding varieties.

QUEEN MARY ROSE GARDEN, REGENT'S PARK, LONDON (Plate 232).

This garden was first conceived in 1932 as a National Rose Garden, but in 1935 Her Majesty Queen Mary gave her gracious permission for it to be called the Queen Mary Rose Garden, and it has now become famous under that name. In recent years it has been redesigned and greatly extended under the expert direction of the Superintendent, Mr S. M. Gault, and during the summer attracts many thousands of visitors from all over the world.

ROSERAIE DE L'HAŸ-LES-ROSES, SCEAUX, PARIS (Plate 235).

La Roseraie de l'Haÿ-les-Roses, near Paris, was created in 1893 for Jules Gravereaux, who conceived the ambition to collect together all the varieties grown for the Empress Joséphine at the beginning of that century at the Château de Malmaison. There is here a wonderful display of all the old roses, carefully labelled and segregated into their proper classes, and of the newer ones right down to modern times. A specially built chalet also houses here a museum devoted to roses and rose-lore.

ROSETO DI ROMA (Plate 239).

In 1928, on the ruins of the Domus Aurea, the Palace of the Emperor Nero, there was planted a new municipal garden in which roses were predominant. This feature was further extended in 1948 on a new site astride the Via Murcia, on Mount Aventino. Here, in a great amphitheatre, are now over a thousand old and new varieties planted in the wide-spreading semicircular beds. On the other side of the road is the international test garden, where world-wide raised new roses are planted and judged at the annual 'Concorso' by an international jury. A Gold Medal and other valuable prizes are awarded.